NEXT-LEVEL ALLY

How to Support Your Queer & Transgender Friends

ELI SACHSE

Microcosm Publishing
Portland, OR | Cleveland, OH

NEXT—LEVEL ALLY

How to Support Your Queer & Transgender Friends

MICROCOSM PUBLISHING is Portland's most diversified publishing house and distributor, with a focus on the colorful, authentic, and empowering. Our books and zines have put your power in your hands since 1996, equipping readers to make positive changes in their lives and in the world around them. Microcosm emphasizes skill-building, showing hidden histories, and fostering creativity through challenging conventional publishing wisdom with books and bookettes about DIY skills, food, bicycling, gender, self-care, and social justice. What was once a distro and record label started by Joe Biel in a drafty bedroom was determined to be *Publishers Weekly*'s fastest-growing publisher of 2022 and #3 in 2023, and is now among the oldest independent publishing houses in Portland, OR, and Cleveland, OH. Biel is also the winner of PubWest's Innovator Award in 2024. We are a politically moderate, centrist publisher in a world that has inched to the right for the past 80 years.

NEXT-LEVEL ALLY

How to Support Your Queer & Transgender Friends

ELI SACHSE

CONTENTS

SO, YOU THINK YOU'RE AN ALLY?

Ally: One that is associated with another as a helper: a person or group that provides assistance and support in an ongoing effort, activity, or struggle (e.g., a political ally.)

—Merriam-Webster

You're conscious. You're conscientious. You vote. You have queer and transgender friends and read about their struggles, and you sympathize. You encourage and say nice things to your queer and trans friends in private or in direct messages. You don't say hateful things. You want to call yourself an ally, but you have the strong feeling you could be doing more. But where to start? The world is so messed up right now and you feel powerless.

Maybe you make your best attempt to honor your queer and trans friends' requests, but you feel like you sometimes fail, though you're not really sure. Sometimes you upset them and their frustration comes completely out of the blue. You were really trying to be nice! You were trying to use the pronouns and terms they prefer, but they ended up having to correct you again. Or, you were trying to stand up for them during a family discussion, but they ended up frustrated and embarrassed instead. Maybe you told a joke you thought for sure was funny and harmless, but they didn't take it the right way.

I've got bad news for you: *you're not an ally . . . yet.* But I've also got good news: this book will point you in loads of possible directions that will help you forge your unique path towards allyship.

I've seen a lot happen in the six years of direct advocacy work I have done in my rural community of Merced, California. California, in many ways, is in a very unique bubble of protection for queer and trans folks, at least compared to the rest of the country and world. However, pockets of rural California have their ultra-nationalist, evangelical, and racist strongholds just like everywhere else in the country. I've given presentations to school administrators who counter back, "We don't have those kinds of students here." (Every school has queer kids. *Gallup* poll data released in 2024[1] shows 22.3% of Gen Z identifies as LGBTQ. It's just a question of whether or not they feel comfortable telling you about it.) We've had a local effort to counter Pride celebrations with a "straight Pride" parade organized by white supremacist groups, which ended up being shut down through counter-protest efforts. Our local queer community has been deeply divided by multiple organizations going after the same buckets of local grant money, and the resulting fractures make progress difficult. This is a common problem in communities across the country, large and small.

So, even in California, there is a lot to be done, and a lot that

1 J. M. Jones, "LGBTQ+ Identification in U.S. Now at 7.6%," *Gallup*, March 13, 2024, https://news.gallup.com/poll/611864/lgbtq-identification.aspx.

you can help with.

In addition to being an advocate and community activist, I'm a registered nurse. I've worked in a transgender clinic that was part of a large health center, serving around 200 transgender patients in 2016-2018. I've worked as a home health nurse, hospice nurse, mental health case manager, and public health nurse. With the American Red Cross, I deployed to disaster recovery efforts as a health services supervisor, organizing teams of volunteers. As a transgender person, I have received good care, incredulity, and refusal from healthcare providers, good advice and bad advice, and I've interacted with nonprofits and health care systems on both coasts of the United States. Because of all of these experiences, I have seen a lot of ally-led actions that work, and others that don't.

I've seen firsthand how well-meaning people have taken power from local queers and thus divided the community. I've seen straight allies take control of queer organizations through political power and maneuvering. This resulted in a (probably inevitable) fracture in the community between queers who insist on queer leadership, and those who think that muting queer or revolutionary voices in favor of political power is strategic (aka respectability politics). And I've seen larger organizations in neighboring communities with robust grant writing resources take money away from the local community here in Merced.

But I've also seen work done by allies that has made all the difference. I worked with cis doctors and nurse practitioners who used their power to make their clinics better for trans people, fighting for processes that ensure we are addressed with respect and receive the unique and trauma-informed care we need. I have been touched by friends and family who have stood up for and affirmed me personally during my gender transition journey of the last ten years. I know that LGBTQ cultural sensitivity education has improved over the years, as I've been exposed to it in many different workplaces on both coasts, and I know that means that someone, in some HR department somewhere, advocated for it. And I've worked with editors, producers, business owners, and project managers who are committed to uplifting queer voices and creating queer spaces and opportunities.

I probably don't have to tell you this, but your queer, trans, and non-binary friends need your help right now in a big way. We face discrimination and phobia on a daily basis, from getting passed over for jobs because it might be "too complicated" to verbal slurs to the microagressions we face just moving around in this world as gender non-conforming people. People stare, trying to gender us mentally. On the train, in the bathroom. They wonder if we belong there. They silently accuse us of "perversion." You might be familiar with some of these hostile looks. And studies are showing that this rain of minor but daily stresses takes years from peoples' lives. A quick Google of "minority stress" will show you plenty of science on the subject.

This book begins with some fundamental concepts that support allyship, namely radical empathy and how to become more confident about speaking up about injustice. It will help you navigate when to speak up and when to let your queer and trans friends take the stage themselves. I'll give you thought exercises about your specific workplace and community so you can start to strategize about how to make the biggest impact where you're at. I'll also talk specifically about talking to relatives, kids, and workmates. And I'll give you ideas about ways you can support (or create) events and opportunities for queer people in your area which enhances visibility and safety for all.

Every ally's journey is different because everyone's skills, local community needs, and access to resources are different. But this book gives tons of concrete, real-life examples and actionable steps you can use in all kinds of different scenarios.

Why Now? Trans People Are Under Attack

As of the writing of this book, according to the ACLU, 74 laws discriminating against LGBTQ people were passed in 2025 in the United States.[2] They run the gamut from outlawing transgender medical care to prohibiting trans teens from playing sports in school or using the correct restroom and locker room to outlawing DEI initiatives. On January 20, 2025, Executive Order 14168 prohibited the recognition of transgender people on government websites.

While it might be tempting to dismiss some executive orders as hollow posturing, it is important to note that one very real result is they embolden the states already proposing and enacting discriminatory laws, especially those states that are particularly targeting trans teens. Discriminatory executive orders condone hate, thus deepening the divide between the states that are enforcing and codifying LGBTQ discrimination and those that are not. Just the thing we need right now.

Meanwhile, other executive orders have immediate consequences. On January 27, 2025, Executive Order 14183 banned transgender people from serving in the military. Service

_____

2 "Mapping Attacks on LGBTQ Rights in U.S. State Legislatures in 2025," *American Civil Liberties Union,* January 15, 2025, https://www.aclu.org/legislative-attacks-on-lgbtq-rights-2025.

members immediately lost their careers, regardless of how many years of service they had provided.

> A note on the language I'm using in this book: 2025 felt like drowning in a tsunami of experimental hate language from our federal and state politicians as they maligned and attacked transgender people with invented terms and pseudoscience. I don't use any of these kinds of terms in this book, therefore I also do not mention specific legislation and other tactics by name. In this book, I am intentionally modeling good, kind, and correct language to arm allies who are not yet confident about speaking about queer issues with the right things to say. Queer theory may be new to you and that's OK! Affirming language is not taught in all schools and is not always modeled on TV; give yourself time and grace while you learn the language of tolerance.

The federal government has other ways to wield immediate and absolute power. For example, in 2025, the federal government ordered federal agents to destroy the passports of non-binary people renewing passports with an X gender marker (as opposed to M or F), instead issuing ones with their assigned birth gender. There is ample evidence of this on social media, where people with an X gender marker who applied for passport renewal have received their old passport back destroyed (holes punched into the side). As of this writing, the Department of State's travel.state.gov website confirms that they will no longer be issuing X gender marker passports, and will only "issue a passport with an M or F sex marker."

In 2026, I have to renew my own passport. I have spoken with staff at ACLU, who confirm that most transgender people like me are receiving renewed passports marked with their old sex assigned at birth at this time. For myself, I am a transgender man who transitioned a decade ago. This means that when I renew my passport this year, I will likely receive a replacement that features a picture of me with the goatee I pretty much always have on my face, my more angular features, broader shoulders, and a female gender marker. Will this cause problems for me when I visit China? I really don't know.

In February 2026, I met a young transgender woman who told a story about how her inaccurate documents confused the airline employee and they checked her bag under a totally unrelated woman's name! Her bag ended up in another state.

Another tangible result of these anti-trans government actions is that medical facilities all over the country have stopped providing gender-affirming care—especially for youth. This means an uptick in transgender people getting care in neighboring states where it is still offered. From 2016 to 2018, I worked as a nurse providing direct patient care to teens and adults seeking transgender healthcare. At that time, I saw folks crossing state lines to access care simply because there were no providers educated in the practice in their home state. Trans care was still relatively new and rare at that time. As trans care became more widely available in all states the number of people I saw crossing state lines for care diminished.

Now, in my role as an administrator for a local nonprofit that connects people to medical care, I'm seeing it again. I see families with trans teens crossing state lines for care after the care they were receiving in their home state was abruptly cut off due to new legislation. I'm seeing people coming to California before their prescriptions run out. These are the families that have the means to make the trip; thousands of other people and families do not have that ability.

This is a pretty grim picture of what is happening in our communities and our country, but you, the person holding this book, can help. That might sound like an impossible fantasy, but it is true.

There are two very important lessons we have to start with to begin to address and combat all this. First, we need to explore the difference between sympathy and empathy. This will lead us to the very important concept of radical empathy. Second, there is no such thing as a silent ally. To be an ally you have to speak up and act out. The next two chapters will guide you to the ways you can start doing exactly that.

CHAPTER I

SYMPATHY VERSUS RADICAL EMPATHY

Maybe you're already past this. But I have to start at the very beginning to make sure we are all on the same page.

First and foremost, we all have to agree that there is injustice in the world. Because just like some people think that feminism is unnecessary because they believe that women have the same shot as anyone at success today (which is wrong, research shows that women still earn less and are in positions of power less often than men), there are some people who argue that queer justice, LGBTQ-focused events and spaces, and other protections are not necessary in this day and age. They find them intrusive or accuse queer people of "pushing our sexuality in their faces" or being attention whores. They argue that taking up social space is not necessary or is even counter-productive.

Well, I hope you know that this is wrong, and that there is still a long way to go on the road to equality. Women, people of color, disabled people, older people, younger people, they all face unequal treatment in most systems in our current society. And queer, trans, non-binary, and intersex people are definitely in this category. Even if you think that queer people and people of color in urban areas go through most days without direct, vocal attacks (which isn't true for everyone, though some do), you still have to consider the millions of people in rural areas who face silent hatred and unspoken hurdles, and the facts of institutionalized racism and injustice.

It might seem off topic, but beefing up your conversational skills about justice in general is a prerequisite for talking about queer justice confidently.

Structural Inequities Are Real

Institutionalized racism and injustice means that marginalized groups face hurdles in their lives that are a result of the very way that society is laid out. This is a provable fact. One illustration of this is the fact that Black people are overwhelmingly, disproportionately incarcerated. This is not merely a symptom of overt racism because there are cops that exist that are not racist and people aren't in jail simply because a cop said a slur (overt racism). Black people are disproportionately incarcerated because there are things about the whole system of policing and prison—for instance, more police presence in communities of color—that make it so that Black people end up in jail more often.[3] It's complicated. But the fact that this is the reality of things is an example of institutionalized or structural racism.

Other examples of institutional injustice are how people of color are disproportionately affected by pollution, are more

3 Becky Pettit and Carmen Gutierrez, "Mass Incarceration and Racial Inequality," *American Journal of Economics and Sociology,* 77, no. 3-4 (2018), https://doi.org/10.1111/ajes.12241.

likely to live in a "food desert," and have less access to nature, all of which can lead to poorer health and shorter lives.[4] Another example is that Black women are more likely to die during childbirth.[5] These realities are not attributable to some individual being directly racist, they exist because this is how the systems in our society are structured.

Queer people are disproportionately affected by mental illness,[6] substance use disorders,[7] domestic and intimate partner violence, sexually transmitted infections, and even certain cancers.[8] They are less likely overall to be connected to primary care than cis straight people, and much more likely to have experienced negative interactions with medical and mental health personnel, and considered, attempted, or completed suicide.[9]

The reasons for all this are varied and layered. But

4 Clare E. B. Cannon, "Critical Environmental Injustice: A Case Study Approach to Understanding Disproportionate Exposure to Toxic Emissions," Toxics, 12, no. 4 (2024), https://doi.org/10.3390/toxics12040295.
5 Marian F. MacDorman et al., "Racial and Ethnic Disparities in Maternal Mortality in the United States Using Enhanced Vital Records, 2016-2017," *American Journal of Public Health*, 111, no. 9 (2021), https://doi.org/10.2105/AJPH.2021.306375.
6 Alex Siu Wing Chan et al., "Investigating the Interrelationships Among Mental Health, Substance Use Disorders, and Suicidal Ideation Among Lesbian, Gay, and Bisexual Adults in the United States: Population-Based Statewide Survey Study," *JMIR Public Health and Surveillance*, 10 (2024), https://doi.org/10.2196/48776.
7 Robert W. S. Coulter et al., "The Effects of Gender- and Sexuality-Based Harassment on Lesbian, Gay, Bisexual, and Transgender Substance Use Disparities," *The Journal of Adolescent Health*, 62, no. 6 (2018), https://doi.org/10.1016/j.jadohealth.2017.10.004.
8 Greta M. Massetti et al., "Public Health Opportunities for Promoting Health Equity in Cancer Prevention and Control in LGBT Populations," *LGBT Health*, 3, no. 1 (2016), doi:10.1089/lgbt.2015.0109.
9 Katherine Bristowe et al., "Recommendations to Reduce Inequalities for LGBT People Facing Advanced Illness: ACCESSCare National Qualitative Interview Study," *Palliative Medicine*, 32, no. 1 (2018), https://doi.org/10.1177/0269216317705102.

researchers who have spent time on the subject agree that some of the reasons are: queer people are less likely to have a strong family support network, more likely to be single and childless, more likely to have developed poor coping mechanisms like substance use due to a history of abuse and ostracism, more likely to have a constellation of mental health challenges that make it difficult to treat any one of them, more susceptible to certain cancers as a result of avoiding primary care visits and genital screenings, and more susceptible to UTI due to avoiding public restrooms.

The variety of injustices that marginalized groups experience in this country is vast. There are many more examples than the ones I mention above. If you aren't part of a minority group, it might be difficult for you to understand the disadvantages they face. You personally may have never faced anything like them. But we have to fight for justice for all people even if we don't, or can't, experience it directly.

In fact, if you have not faced these kinds of hurdles and barriers in your life, you are *uniquely equipped* to be able to fight and speak up about them. Privileged, in fact. This is for a variety of reasons. First, you can speak up without fear of discrimination, stigma, or silencing based on your identity. In the case of transgender people in particular, opponents argue that our identity is not even real or valid; that we are mentally ill, deluded, mistaken. This makes it impossible for us to argue the validity of our own viewpoints. You might also find yourself in a more professionally and financially stable position from which to argue and take a stand. And you are more likely to hold a position of real power and influence.

I believe that with this privilege comes the responsibility

to consciously, and vocally, do work for justice. Because when we do actual work, and share about why we are doing it and why it is important, we are creating a culture of knowledge and empowerment. By spreading the word about the work we are doing and the things we are learning, either actively by telling the story or passively as people observe what we are building, we spread tolerance, understanding, and empathy as a natural consequence.

This might sound a bit utopian and idyllic, but it really is true. Research is showing that some of the most effective ways of fighting hatred and inequality are education and sharing stories in the spirit of cultivating *radical empathy*.

Sympathy Is Not Enough

To talk about empathy, we have to talk about sympathy. Sympathy means you *feel bad* for your friend. You are sympathetic when you say, "Wow, I'm so sorry your cat died." You feel bad, but you might not have a full understanding about how your friend feels if you've never experienced something like that yourself. Your statement actually implies that. People send sympathy cards that say "Get Well Soon!" or "My Condolences." But these hollow, pre-printed messages are pretty devoid of personal meaning. But, while that's better than nothing, it really isn't a substitute for empathy, which is something totally different.

Empathy is *understanding* how your friend feels. You can empathize with their broken leg because you also broke your leg when you were little. You can empathize with their family struggles because your family is messed up, too. But is that the only way you can experience empathy?

Is Real Empathy Possible?

Some people argue that we can never really empathize with someone from a totally different background than us. But I don't believe this is true. It's like people who argue that some words or concepts are untranslatable into different languages like *hygge* or *umami*. But this isn't true, either. It just takes more work, and more words.

For example, *umami* is a Japanese word that loosely translates into "savory," but that's not a perfect translation. In English, "savory" is used to describe anything that isn't sweet. Umami more specifically refers to our perception of amino acids and proteins. This roughly means things that we find meaty, like a rich broth, gravy, mushroomy, or marrow kind of flavor profile or fermented foods like soy sauce or Vegemite. English doesn't have one word for this flavor. So, it takes a little extra time to conceptualize what umami is for an English speaker, but it is not impossible.

It's the same with empathizing with different cultures, backgrounds, and the struggles of others. It takes a fuck-ton more work than just reading an article about it. For example, I didn't really get the concept of institutionalized racism until I took a semester-long sociology class regarding race and gender disparities. As in: I really just didn't get it, for like, months. But just because something is hard, doesn't mean it is impossible or not worthwhile. I'd argue that it makes it *especially* worthwhile. I *want* a deeper understanding of lots of things. And I accept that this takes a lot of work and time.

I first heard about radical empathy on a radio program on *NPR* sometime before the 2016 American presidential election.

People with very different, and hostile, political views were put into groups of two, asked to very carefully listen to the other's story, and then describe it from a first-person point of view to the group afterwards. They had to learn how to act and speak as the other, to a certain degree.

One of the pairs was a very conservative person paired with a transgender man. We got to listen to snippets of their conversation, where the transgender man explained how the identity he felt most strongly aligned with at that moment was his role as a father. A nerve was hit, and the conservative person described his surprise at how this forced him to realize their shared humanity. When the time came for everyone to tell their partner's story to the group, you could tell that just using the term "transgender" was new to the conservative person. But he conscientiously made the effort to use the correct term.

This is radical empathy. It means you have listened to, and taken to heart, the feelings and lived experience of another. You have taken the time to find parallels in your own life and feelings of your own that might match in some way. You have found an appreciation for the struggles of another, accessed some understanding about their situation, and have started to think about ways you might be able to help alleviate some of the burden. It takes a whole lot of work—talking *and* listening. But unfortunately, there is no good substitute.

Making Stories Real

One way to build empathy, in little steps throughout our every days, is to talk about queer issues—incessantly. This is because no one has a perfect understanding of everything. Not even queer people. There is always something to be learned from someone different from us. And since not everyone in the world happens to have close queer or trans friends (at least ones that they know about) we have to work to make them a part of the everyday conversation.

This doesn't mean gossiping about the personal lives of your queer and trans friends at every opportunity, of course. It can mean a lot of other things. Ultimately, your justice conversations will be unique to your experiences, location, and audience.

For you, this might look like inserting queer and trans lives into conversations with your family, if that's a place where queer and trans lives don't normally come up in conversation. Mention a happy life milestone of a queer coworker or fellow queer student. Mention a queer wedding that you are considering attending. Mention how you feel proud and happy about a celebrity or politician coming out publicly. Bring up a local piece of legislation that is meant to protect or deny the rights of queer and trans people in your area. Discuss who proposed the bill, who supports it, who is against it, and why. Talk about why it matters.

Mention that a Pride celebration is coming up in your area, and invite your family to go with you. Maybe your family thinks they don't know anyone personally who is queer, so why would they go? Tell them it doesn't matter; Pride celebrations are about equality and safety for everyone, and it is important for the whole community to show up and celebrate.

At work, this might look like bringing up a news item that has to do with queer or trans people, and explaining to your coworkers why the issue is important to a lot of people, and to you. Maybe you have the opportunity to talk about a new, queer-owned business in your town. You could offer commentary to colleagues about how you are excited about the business and wishing for the success of all LGBTQ-led initiatives. We will cover more ways you can speak out in detail in later chapters.

This will take courage and practice. It means being brave enough to talk about things people might find controversial. It means speaking out for what you believe in. It means creating a future where these things will no longer be considered controversial. We normalize things by talking about them. By making them real, local, touchable.

And Don't Forget to Listen

And the flipside; we also have to incessantly *listen*. We have to seek out trans and queer stories. This can become the heart of an intentional practice. Since the culture and availability of care and connection is constantly changing in this country, queer and trans people are having to continually adapt and shift. This means inventing new language for the things we are experiencing and realizing, and chronicling our ever-evolving stories. Cultivate a daily or weekly practice of listening. Watch queer-made and queer-focused movies, shows, and shorts, listen to podcasts, read articles and books by queer authors, seek out news on queer justice and injustice in this country and around the world. Listening is a crucial component to the cycle of listening and speaking up. And you're building up an ever more complete and nuanced vocabulary of radical empathy in the process.

The more content you absorb, and the more talking you do about it, the more confident you naturally become at speaking up. You may not feel like you have the right vocabulary down yet. That means it's time to listen to the wide variety of queer-made content out there, right now. Then you can practice using it. Start with posting about it on socials. Then, practice with a few good friends. Graduate to workmates. Then family. Rinse, and repeat.

Developing and strengthening your radical empathy and your listening skills will go a long way to creating the foundation of your allyship. See the Resources list at the end of the book for great places to listen to queer stories like *Making Gay History* and *StoryCorps*. Visit your local library's ebook and audiobook collection, too, and pick up a book on radical empathy.

CHAPTER 2

THERE IS NO SUCH THING AS A SILENT ALLY

Nonintervention does not mean that nothing happens.

—Christopher Hitchens

Your queer, trans, and non-binary friends need your help, especially those in the closet who are fearful of coming out. As I say in the previous chapter, you are actually in a unique position to fight for justice for them, specifically because you don't face the same daily hurdles. You will not face the same social consequences for speaking out that they might. Just like women who speak out loudly about feminism can be unjustly painted as shrill and uppity, and in this way are silenced, your diverse friends face a variety of stigma and opposition when trying to speak out for themselves. We can be accused of being perverse, pushy, and of polluting the minds of children. The range of things we are accused of is infinite. And this is how we are silenced, how empathy-building is prevented, and ignorance perpetuated.

If we are on top, we have the responsibility to reach a hand down to those below. This means being visible—putting yourself out there. Merely offering your kind words of support in a private message does not help change society. We have to speak out clearly and publicly.

Later chapters will get into lots of ways you can speak out confidently and creatively. But first, let's talk about language, visibility, and some recent history that brought us to the current moment.

When Language Creation Exploded

The social conversation about the transgender experience has opened up in a fast and dramatic way. Only in the last few decades did people start creating the language to even talk about trans and non-binary people, pansexual people, asexual and aromantic people, and their experiences. We've started talking about graysexuality, demisexuality, and omnisexuality. These terms did not exist forty years ago. As this language develops, more and more queer people begin to learn about themselves, our history, and our rights in general. As more people transitioned, after *realizing* they could transition, more trans people began to talk about their stories publicly. And this has created a huge snowball effect. When more queer people become visible, more feel safe coming out.

The change has been so rapid and so dramatic, it is actually little wonder that the old-fashioned folks are feeling confused, left behind, and are pushing back dramatically.

Reclaiming Our Transgender Moment

I think it's important to stress that language and visibility created this new culture of knowledge and safety that we find

ourselves in—compared to twenty years ago, or even ten. This is exactly why I transitioned at the age of thirty-six. For most of my life, I didn't know that there were guys that transitioned permanently; I had never heard or seen their stories. I didn't have half of the vocabulary that I've been using throughout this book.

For most of my life, I thought that my only option was to be an eternal "tomboy" or "butch," the only language I knew that came close to describing what I was while I was growing up and well into adulthood. I always felt like a guy, but who could I talk to about that in the 1980s? No one. As a child, actually around age six, seven, or eight, I distinctly remember thinking that I ought to have a little boy's body. And I remember thinking immediately after, "Clearly, this makes me a pervert, and I can never tell anyone about it." I don't know where I got that language from. But I didn't talk to anyone about it for more than twenty years. I simply didn't have the ability to.

I knew drag queens—men who performed as women on weekends, and then went back to work in a suit and tie on Mondays. But their experience didn't seem to have anything to do with mine. I had no desire to perform.

Then, somewhere around 2011, I finally started hearing the national conversation about transgender people. I started seeing stories about guys like me. At that point, I found I just couldn't go back. There were words now for what I was. Words that explained my whole life experience. From there, I could begin to see how to craft a plan forward. In fact, once I realized that people transitioned permanently, I just about simultaneously realized that I simply couldn't go on living my life without having *tried.*

The Impact of the Affordable Care Act

I also think it isn't talked about enough, nor even widely recognized, that President Obama and the Affordable Care Act (ACA) had a huge hand in bringing about this reality. In 2012, the ACA mandated that transgender care be covered by insurance in the United States. Medicare, state Medicaid plans, and private insurers all fell into line with relative swiftness and lack of protest, and began to cover trans care across the country. To me, this was the event that truly kicked over the now unstoppable snowball of visibility for transgender people in all facets of our society.

The word "transgender" was essentially invented in the 1990s. Before that, there were only the slurs "trannie," "transexual" (which some have reclaimed as a positive identity, but that's relatively rare), and the loosely related cross-dresser, drag queen, and drag king. Now, some lucky teens even have access to trans medical care and affirming parents encouraging them to live their best lives. They are playing sports, being elected to student leadership, and being prom kings and queens. There are trans and non-binary actors, doctors, surgeons, spiritual leaders, teachers, scientists, politicians, military personnel. We are everywhere people are.

I feel profoundly lucky, dumbfounded really, to be able to be witnessing this sea change in real time. In 2015, *CNN* reported on "America's transgender moment"[10] and in some ways, it feels like the momentum has never slowed.

The Hateful Book

Then in 2018, a hateful book and essay based on pseudoscience

10 Brandon Griggs, "America's Transgender Moment," *CNN*, April 23, 2015, https://www.cnn.com/2015/04/23/living/transgender-moment-jenner-feat/.

called *When Harry Became Sally: Responding to the Transgender Moment* was released. Hateful religious groups like the Heritage Foundation co-opted the phrase "transgender moment" in order to try to reframe this generational, cultural movement into a "fad," a passing aberration. Unfortunately, malicious results flood a Google search for "transgender moment" right now.

However, I feel it is important to recognize 2012-2015 for the cultural revolution that access to trans care started, access that President Obama and all those who fought for the ACA are ultimately responsible for. This is not just to give credit where credit is due, but to recognize that our transgender moment was not a quirk, a random happenstance, or a great coincidence. Rather, it happened because of real events and very clever advocates who realized their chance to codify trans rights in the biggest and most impactful way in our country's history.

Our transgender moment did *not* happen because of social media influencers with a secret agenda targeting kids, foreign agents, chemicals in the water, vaccinations, or whatever other fantasies conspiracy fans will throw at you. It was because people spoke up, and made change.

Knowing our history empowers you with the truth to counter false narratives and is fundamental to your next-level ally education.

LGBTea

CHAPTER 3

UNGENDER YOUR ASSUMPTIONS

I am a big fan of gender-neutral language. I think that the world will be a better place when the majority of languages have no gender assumptions. Just to be clear, this isn't to say that we can never talk about gender, sex, genitals, or anything associated with them ever again. There are times and places where that is definitely applicable.

What I'm talking about here are *assumptions*. Like when we are first meeting and greeting someone.

For example, when you have a trans friend, especially one early in transition, gendering them correctly and publicly *can* feel good and affirming. Going out of your way to affirm your trans friend's gender is being a next-level ally. Everyone will be different, but I really appreciate language that exaggerates, even ridiculously, my gender. I like dude, "Broseph!," homie, brother, "the gentleman," sir, *chulo*, *mijo*, and *guapo*. I go out of my way to affirm my trans lady friends with "Hey, ladies," girls, babes, ma'am. This, of course, varies from person to person, and you

33

will have to experiment with trial and error, and humor, among your close friends.

But in other situations, especially involving strangers or acquaintances, I really think that gender-neutral is the way to go, the way of the future.

Think about it: what are you doing when you address a stranger as "ma'am"? You are assuming their gender.

They/Them Pronouns Remove Gender Assumptions

Not all trans people feel this way, but I actually feel good and affirmed when cafe staff address me as "they." This signals that they aren't assuming anything. That there may be a question about my gender, but it is not a problem or a topic of conversation. I feel seen, and also normalized. However, other trans people can get offended if they are "they-ed" by a customer service person.

I can see their point. For example, a trans person who has invested a lot of time and money into their appearance, clothing, shoes, suit, dress, accessories, and more, *really, really* wants you to see them as the gender they present (refer back to aggressively gendering trans friends in an affectionate way). With strangers, sometimes this can be a nice thing, too. For example, when I see someone who I feel might be a transgender woman, I will sometimes go out of my way to compliment her bag or hair, or say to her "your makeup is just so on point." This can feel really good to a stranger. For gender non-conforming strangers I meet, I often say "I just love your whole look," gesturing to everything about them. This can be a wonderful practice.

But, these are pretty specific examples that involve people

you might not meet everyday. So, for the most part, I don't see anything wrong with people in a public role using gender-neutral pronouns and terms 99% of the time. If you think about it—and try it—you'll see that it removes assumptions and becomes very easy in a short time. And it eliminates mistakes!

To be clear, the mistake in this situation is gendering the customer or stranger *incorrectly*. (Calling a trans woman "he.") It's hard to describe how existentially sad and disappointing this feels early on in one's transition.

Mistakes

I have made them. We all have! We apologize briefly, not making a scene, and move on. For me, having worked in a transgender clinic, seeing nothing but transgender patients all evening, and running trans support groups and LGBTQ nonprofits—I have interacted with an outsized number of trans people in my life. In the clinic, I saw almost no one except trans people early in their transition and it was either using they/them or mistake after mistake. So, for me, when doing this work, I have settled on the practice of defaulting to them/them pronouns in every setting. That's just how it's been for me. Your mileage may vary.

I think that in the future, even medical forms will eliminate gender related questions because they really are unnecessary. Sure, there are some body parts that are unique to certain genders. But these are easily talked about in private, and in neutral language, between provider and patient. There is no reason for *front office staff* to ask a person's gender. I'd argue that it is private and protected health information.

How much more true is this for the DMV, social security, job applications, credit card applications? What does one's gender matter in these circumstances? Not at all, of course. Unless you are a company or entity that is intent on discrimination. Did you know that many major orchestras now use a blind audition method and this has *significantly increased* the hiring of women musicians?[11]

Also, by using they/them pronouns for everyone and everything, you are normalizing the experience of your non-binary friends. They become part of the majority, instead of a minority and a curiosity. And why not? There is simply no reason to not use gender-neutral language everywhere and everyday.

And by the way, to the cis people who have removed their gender information from social media, so that you are referred to as "they" by the system, I see you. And I appreciate you. I like that.

Again, this is not to say that we can't talk about gender or pee-pees, manscaping or vajazzling with our friends ever again. It's about knowing your audience, which is simply another way of saying *being respectful*. Maybe the following table can help.

---

11 Claudia Goldin and Cecilia Rouse, "Orchestrating Impartiality: The Impact of "Blind" Auditions on Female Musicians," *American Economic Review*, 90, no. 4 (September 2000), https://www.aeaweb.org/articles?id=10.1257/aer.90.4.715.

Gender-Neutral and Inclusive Language

No	Yes
Miss, ma'am, sir, ladies, gentlemen (in a customer service setting)	Folks, friends, or simply "Good evening" or "Welcome"
Ladies and gentlemen (addressing a crowd)	Distinguished guests, gentlefolk, gentlebeings
Waiter/Waitress	Server
Ms./Mrs./Mr. (written)	Mx.
Sir/Ma'am/Miss/Missus (spoken)	This is the hardest one. We don't have a formal substitute ready for the folks who expect these terms in certain settings. Everyone has to assess their profession and setting and create the language that feels right for them. I address clients as "friends" because in my job my intent is to establish rapport quickly and the medical setting is becoming less formal everyday. But this may not feel right for you. Putting extra emphasis on the "Good evening," with intentional and respectful eye-contact and a nod, and leaving off the rest can work. You are going to create your own style.

He/Him, She/Her	They/Them or use first names, nicknames, or descriptions: "The person in the pink sweatshirt." "The person with the short hair."
Mom and dad	Parents, guardians, "your folks"
Girlfriend, boyfriend, husband, wife	Friend, partner, life partner, spouse, sweetheart
Brothers, sisters, aunts, uncles, cousins	Siblings, nibblings, kin, family
My dudes,* my ladies, my girls	My people, my friends
Boys and girls	Children, kids, kiddos, littles, teenagers

*Sidenote: In California, debate continues to rage on whether or not "dude" is gender-neutral. For myself, I have a large proportion of friends who are transwomen and they object to the term, seeing it as masculine. Therefore, I personally don't use it in a gender-neutral way anymore because I can't be trusted to use it in different ways with different audiences. That's just me.

Practice, Practice, Practice

Inclusive language gets fun and easy over time, I promise. But it does take practice.

I also think that we all could use *affectionate nicknames* more often, and these can easily be tailored to be inclusive, affirming, and neutral. Have fun with this!

I use they/them pronouns in everyday language, even when referring to cis people, actually. I think it is a great way to interrupt people's speech patterns and to get them to consider what they are saying. It also gets people used to the sound of they/them in conversation. As should be obvious by now, I almost always refer to people I haven't met yet with they/them. Because I want to signal to people that you cannot assume gender identity from a name.

Just to be clear, yes, I have used "Hey, guys" and other gendered language over the course of this book. Gender is a thing. We talk about it, sometimes. We don't have to drastically alter the way we speak to remove gender from 100% of the things we say immediately, that is not what I am suggesting. That would be a bit weird, and opposed to what we want to be doing which is making gradual and natural changes in our environments that eventually make *everyone* feel less weird.

What we want to think about removing are *assumptions*. That is what gender-neutral pronouns, office forms, letters, and greetings accomplish. There are so many reasons to use they/them and other gender-neutral language everyday. It is something so powerful you can simply choose to start doing right now.

You may be feeling like I am talking about this quite a lot. I'm doing this because removing unnecessary gender from language is helpful for our queer and trans friends, but I'm also doing it to give you the language to explain to others why gender-neutral language is important, easy, and ultimately not a big deal.

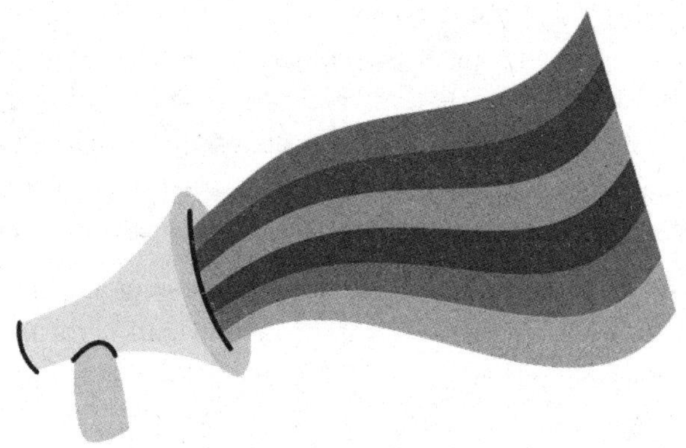

CHAPTER 4

APOLOGIZE, INTERJECT, CORRECT

Everything in this book is useful for being a strong ally for your trans and non-binary friends. But it is equally useful for your bisexual friends, aromantic friends, your coworkers in polyamourous relationships, your colleagues in relationships with gender non-conforming people—basically, anyone who is traditionally silenced and erased from the conversation.

People can be erased by the very way that our language and common conversations are constructed. In this chapter, we will take a deep dive into analyzing the conversational patterns we engage in everyday, and how to make them more inclusive for all people.

Queer the Conversation

Heteronormative conversations exclude gay people. As queer people, we sit there listening to the seemingly endless conversations and flat jokes about heterosexual relationship culture (Men are from Mars . . .), heteronormative marriages and family milestones, offspring being had, celebrated, and cared for, and may think to ourselves, "Well, that has never happened to me, and may never happen to me." And so we are not part of the conversation. We have no opening, no opportunity to share something similar.

To be clear, some queer couples opt for offspring, extended family, marriage, mortgages, and the like. But there are an equal if not greater number of us who simply have no interest in such things. Include in this category older queers who grew up without the possibility of these things in their future (marriage having been illegal). So, for a lot of us, we have never even stopped to imagine these things. They were never things we felt we *could* aspire to. And there are plenty of young queers who reject nuclear family culture as a matter of principle or choice.

Sometimes we have the energy to be courageous and challenge the conversation with a fabulous corollary. Like interjecting into a conversation about a stag party a comment about including male escorts. But other times, we are just tired and stay quiet. Even your queer friends who you might think of as boisterous and fearless, have many times throughout the day stayed silent, and were thus left out, for a host of reasons. We are furthermore erased when we simply do not feel comfortable participating in the conversation because of hateful or uneducated things that are said. We don't want to be the sole voice, visibly different, outnumbered by hate and heteronormativity. Sometimes we stay silent because we worry that challenging the conversation is going to end up forcing us to explain or defend something personal.

With this in mind, be intentional about bringing your queer

friends and colleagues into the conversation. If thirty minutes of your lunch break have been taken up with conversation about a baby shower, menstruation, and makeup (or other heavily binary-gendered topics), or children and childcare when you know your colleague is childless, make some kind of effort to draw them into conversation. Talk about movies, gardening, news, any topic you know or suspect they might be interested in. Ask them about their weekend plans. Ask them about their partner, if you know they are open at work about their partner and romantic life.

Steer It Away from the Personal When Needed

Some of your colleagues and friends might not be totally in the closet, meaning they might not be secretive about the entirety of their identity. But at the same time, they might not be comfortable with sharing 100% of the details about their personal life with everyone in the workplace or friend group.

Maybe they feel comfortable with some people or some details but not others. Maybe they are afraid that their sexual identity will overshadow other parts of their personality with certain people who haven't had a lot of exposure to queers. Maybe they are just a private person.

With that in mind, don't be the person that uncomfortably *presses* a queer person to answer personal questions in a group setting. Rather, attempt to draw them into a conversation without putting them on the spot. And, if necessary, interrupt others who are putting the queer on the spot. Let them know by saying, "They don't have to answer that" or "You're being very rude/presumptive/nosy asking that!"

Explain Trans Identities . . . When You Can

This one is very much a case-by-case basis kind of thing.

You should definitely let the transgender person tell their own story and share their personal experience when they are comfortable doing so. Everyone's trans journey is unique, so we all have our own perspective on each issue. If your friend, colleague, or family member is very comfortable and willing to explain their story, the surgeries they've had, the relationships they've had, evidenced by them sharing openly with a group, that is a *great thing* and should not be interrupted.

However, there are some situations and conversations where your trans friend might want you to interject on their behalf, particularly when among people they aren't close with, don't know yet, or may not fully trust like work colleagues or distant family. In these cases, if you see your trans friend becoming uncharacteristically shy, nervous, or uncomfortable, it may be a situation where they would be grateful for you interrupting a line of personal questioning coming from someone else.

If you witness someone being pushy about asking if your friend or family member has had "the surgery yet," please do interrupt. Remind the table that this is a "very personal question," not appropriate for the dinner table or lunchroom.

You probably have never experienced a stranger visibly furrowing their brow as they try to imagine which kinds of genitals you have or attempt to form assumptions about how you have sex. But once you see it, the train of thought becomes painfully obvious, and you'll instantly recognize the look next time. Sometimes, this person won't just silently try to guess, they will question directly.

"So, what are you, anyways?" "Are you a man or a woman?" "I'm just asking." Be clear that this is hateful speech, meant to intimidate, humiliate, and silence others.

As a cis ally, you can and should interrupt this train of thought with any conversational tactic that feels right to you. Trans and queer people can be shamed and othered when we are forced to explain the nature of our own sexuality, genitals, gender, or relationships to hostile people. Speak up and face ridicule, rejection, or attack? Or stay quiet, leave, and feel further and further apart from society? This is why a next-level ally makes it their job to do the explaining and educating, or redirecting, whichever makes sense.

In an ideal world, you and your queer or trans friend have pre-gamed the situation and come to an agreement about what level of personal sharing they are comfortable with at said event or place. The answer may be complicated if the person is not yet out to some of their family or workmates, but are out to others. More on this in later chapters.

Don't Let Misgendering Go Unchallenged

As mentioned earlier, the first, ideal step is to talk in private with your trans friend and ask them what pronouns they like to use in public and in private. Their pronouns may differ from public to private if they don't feel safe in their community! Or if they aren't out to family members. Ask them if they would like you to correct mutual friends when they get misgendered. Ask them if they would like you to correct people if they get misgendered in public by strangers. The answer may be different. For example, someone trying on a new gender identity might wish that you do speak up for them when among friends, but feel uncomfortable with the idea of making a scene in public.

Personally speaking, it was one of the most wonderful and freeing things for me to hear other people stepping up on my behalf when I was misgendered early on. I don't get misgendered very much anymore, as I have been living my life as a man now for about nine years, and am seldom mistaken for a woman. However, this was not the case early on.

Those of us early in transition are in an especially vulnerable place. We have decided to tell the world our gender is different. However, it takes time for hormone therapy to do its magic and change our bodies and voices. And for trans women, hormone therapy does not change your voice. Only months and years of voice training can do that. So at the earliest steps, kind of literally nothing has happened except we have told the world what's in our hearts. And then, we are expected to step into the opposite restroom! This is a terrifying prospect which ends up being a process for most people. Few have the courage to step in on that first day. It takes loads of mental preparation. That's why finding out *how* to step in on behalf of folks in this crucial beginning phase of transition is so important.

Some people assume that it is best to let a conversational "slip up" slip by with no commentary to avoid making a fuss, a further discussion, or ruffle any feathers. But the opposite is true. Being misgendered stings. It stings when it is said. It plays on existing anxieties in a hundred different ways. And it stings that you didn't help me.

For me, it would have been such a relief if more people had stepped in on my behalf to correct my other friends and acquaintances. It is exhausting trying to read each situation to see if I will be safe if I speak up or if I will just be made to feel further singled out and ostracized. It was hard to marshal the energy to step in, to interrupt, in what was such a daily occurrence, especially early in my transition. So, I got tired and let people misgender me, and it hurt. Furthermore, ignoring it doesn't help it *stop happening.* The only way to get it to stop happening is to kindly, repeatedly educate people.

When you speak up for me, you are doing the educating for me. You are signaling yourself as a strong ally and are normalizing my situation for anyone in earshot.

That feels so good.

Even though at this point in my transition my close friends rarely misgender me, it still happens. Of course it is an accident, of course they are my good friend whom I know and love, and I know they mean well. But they still screw up. It's equally as important here for you to step in and correct them on my behalf, and not just let it slide. Why? Because letting it slide might signal or reinforce the idea that gendering me correctly is an annoying or impossible chore.

And heck, I of course am not perfect either. I am plenty guilty of misgendering my own friends and acquaintances! When I do, I stop, apologize with very few words, or just one: "Sorry." Use the correct pronoun with clarity and emphasis. And move on.

That's all.

When you ignore misgendering and let it slide instead of apologizing, you may be perpetuating the notion that gendering me correctly is difficult, onerous, or impossible. When nothing could be further from the truth. Human beings are remarkably adaptable, often defaulting to copying the language the group uses, especially if they want to. Therefore, it is so much easier if there is a group of friends using the correct language. Eventually, everyone falls in line and it becomes natural. But in the beginning it might take prodding in the right direction.

Something I feel is useful is to tell my friends that it helps to stop thinking of said person as transgender. Rather, they are simply a man, a woman, or a person, *and they always have been.* You just didn't know it before. Because that is the truth. I am a man, and always have been. I have seen the revelation on people's faces when I explain this to them. You can see something click.

Being a Next-Level Ally Scenario: The Cafe

Say you've talked with your trans friend and gotten explicit permission to speak up when they are misgendered. You both are at a local cafe ordering coffees and when the cashier asks for your order they misgender your friend. What do you do? Simply say to the cashier, "They go by 'them'" or "Actually, it's ma'am." No further explanation is necessary. Most of the time, a customer service worker will simply apologize. Maybe they will be embarrassed. Be gracious. Say "Thanks!" when people respect pronouns, even though it should go without saying. A little grace goes a long way when we are in the beginning stages of changing the world.

But say in this case, you face resistance or hostility. The worker gets defensive, they say something ugly like, "Well, it looked like a 'he' to me." This is where you get to really shine. Recognize comments like these as hostile and transphobic. Comments like these have no place in society today. In most parts of the United States, one's gender identity is a legally protected right and one has the right to demand to be addressed by any name or pronoun they wish. And regardless of whether it is legally protected in your corner of the world, everyone deserves to be called by their right name, to not to be addressed as the wrong gender, and to not be called "it" or any other variety of veiled slur.

With the confidence of this knowledge, challenge the worker. "Well, it doesn't matter what you think. The fact is that my friend is a woman." Depending on the situation, maybe you have the chance to add, "And you owe her an apology." If resistance continues, ask to speak to their manager.

Just to be triply clear, only start causing this kind of fuss once you are 100% positive that your trans friend appreciates you stepping in on their behalf! Look over and check in with them to see how they are doing. Stop if things feel wrong, and move on if necessary.

If your friend is doing OK and is appreciative, explain to the manager that this worker is continuing to insult your friend by calling her a "he." If the manager is also phobic and resistant, politely let them know that you will both be taking your business elsewhere. You might have the energy to add that you will be telling everyone you know that this establishment is hostile, rude, and should be avoided. Maybe they won't care. You shouldn't either. Simply move on.

Before you engage in a scenario like this, you should answer a couple of questions. Is this a place that your friend likes to go to often? If so, are your actions creating a safer space for them to return to or a hostile situation that they might have to face at a later date? There are a lot of variables to consider. This is why pre-gaming with your friend is essential. But you also don't want to overthink yourself into non-action. Remember, you'll often be learning as you go. Also remember, different friends may ask that you show up differently in different situations.

Blast Misgendering Businesses Online

Go ahead and leave an online review, detailing your exact experience in clear, diplomatic language. Explain that the staff was extremely rude or hostile to your friend and you recommend the place be avoided. The comments will often multiply once you are the first to speak out against injustice or disrespectful treatment. This is so helpful in alerting other LGBTQ folks that this place is not a safe space, and to take their business elsewhere.

This example is kind of a worst-case scenario; hopefully you won't encounter it often. Most times, people will acquiesce and apologize. They are, after all, in customer service. Keep in mind that all you are demanding is simple and courteous customer service.

Referencing Gender in the Past Tense

We can misgender transgender people by referring to them as the incorrect gender when speaking about them in the past tense. It is now the accepted norm to refer to our trans friends as *their current gender* when speaking about them in the past, present, and future.

For myself, I was raised as a woman, and I now live my life as a man. You might think, and critics argue, that when talking about me when I was a child, one should use feminine pronouns and refer to me as a little girl. However, speaking this way can pose a few different problems. For one, it makes the conversation awkward, forcing participants to mentally swap genders with each new sentence. This might prove difficult or impossible for some, and prompt clarifying questions. Often, these questions are really irrelevant to the actual conversation, and do nothing except put unnecessary attention and scrutiny on the transgender person.

In the worst-case scenario, speaking about me in the past tense in a different gender outs me to people without my consent. Accordingly, my parents have always had "a son" because explaining it in any other way to a stranger would *out me as trans*.

To me, talking about trans people in this way simply feels disrespectful. It goes back to the idea that I have *always been a boy, you just didn't know it yet*. Depending on the person and the context, hearing people speak about me using the wrong gendered pronouns, even in the past tense, can feel like:

- Broadcasting my strangeness/disgustingness.

- Accentuating our differences (othering me).

- Calling the transgender experience confusing.

- Making it all about the speaker and their experience of my life.

There are some cases when I, as a trans person, choose to out myself, and *describe myself* as having been raised as a girl. But generally speaking, I advise you to leave this particular decision up to the trans person only. Be aware to not conversationally out your trans friend by accident in this way, especially among strangers.

Tell People They're Not Funny

What happens when you hear a homophobic joke? Do you freeze? Politely or nervously laugh? Do you give a chuckle, but with a little snark to try to indicate that the joke was bad? How can you do better here?

It might help to imagine how someone who is the butt of the joke might feel if they were standing right there. It might help to visualize ways that you could courageously stand up for them. You can say in a polite way to someone, "Well, that joke doesn't really work around our gay friends, does it?" You can say this regardless of there being any gay friends present or not. You can make it clear how you feel about jokes like that by saying, "Yeah, not super funny."

The same goes for jokes about polyamory, sex work, or any kind of alternate relationship status.

By saying something like, "That's not funny" or "Don't tell jokes like that," you can shut the banter and joking down, signaling that this topic is closed. Shutting it down can also save someone from having to explain themselves or reveal something about themselves, especially your polyamorous or queer friend who might be sitting right there. Shutting it down might also signal to the joker that they shouldn't assume everyone is straight or cis (more on this in the next chapter).

What if the joker pushes back with something like, "What, are you gay or something?" You may find yourself forced to quickly decide how to respond.

Don't:

- Make eye contact with your queer or sex worker friend. This could be read as outing them (revealing their status).

- Out people who are not present, and who the joker may know.

Do:

- Give a universal answer.

    a. "I don't deal with hate, that's all."

    b. "I already said, it just isn't funny."

    c. "No, it's just that intelligent people don't joke about those kinds of things anymore."

- Out yourself.

    a. "As a matter of fact, I am gay."

- Out people *not present* who you know would be happy to be used as an example.

    b. "I have gay family, coworkers, friends, literally everyone is gay now, dumbass."

Shutting down hateful jokes on our behalf is god's[12] work. Thank you.

---

12 I don't believe in god, but I like the phrase.

Chapter 5

SPEAKING UP AT WORK AND ONLINE

Oh man, have I spoken up at work and online. In this chapter, I will share some of my personal experiences for you to reflect on—take from them what you will. Some things have worked for me, and some have not. I definitely have an appetite for risk that others don't; some scenarios that I see as successful, horrify other people. So, this is not necessarily a blueprint or a roadmap for you. Rather, I share these stories as examples of real-life consequences, both good and bad, in the hopes that they can help you visualize different outcomes that might happen when you start to speak up and take a stand for others.

Two Personal Experiences with Professional Consequences

I am a bisexual, transgender man living in a rural area of America. I know that I have been let go from jobs, and also passed over for opportunities, because of my beliefs and the reality of my life and identity. You might find this surprising, but right now I feel almost happy that this has happened to me so explicitly. This way, I can name it and call it out.

More often, people are silently let go or passed over for opportunities without a tangible reason they can put a finger on. In this scenario there is no recourse to right the wrong. It's kind of like gaslighting. When we are let go without cause, all we can do is sit around and speculate. Lots of times we incorrectly blame ourselves for flubbing the interview or being bad at our job.

For me, I have been passed over for work opportunities at the local hospital because it is run by a Catholic organization. I totally accept the fact that it would probably not be a good fit, as they refuse to prescribe birth control, refer for abortions, or address transgender care. However, over the years, I have occasionally applied for jobs there to test the waters and see if the organization is open to change since the management of it has changed hands several times. My latest interview with them was for a position I was very qualified for and had the relevant experience in. I thought the whole interview was quite positive. I spoke about my experience as a hospice nurse, and how as an atheist I feel comfortable speaking with people of all faiths. I told them, in fact, that I see my atheism as an asset. It's a position that allows me to approach each patient situation without bias, preconception, or unwanted proselytizing. As I spoke, three people on the four-person interview panel nodded at me and said positive things about the relevance of my work experience to the job I was interviewing for.

But then one of the interviewers interjected, stating that part of the mission statement of their organization includes bringing god to the people or something of that nature. And did I feel that was a problem? I said, "No, do *you* feel like that is a problem?" The other interviewers emphatically shook their heads "no," agreeing that there did not seem to be any problem and affirming that I had the appropriate professional outlook on the situation. The person who asked that question stayed silent. I did not get that job offer. To me, it seemed very clear that the only friction appeared when the person questioned my atheism. I could be wrong, but it seems I did not get the job because I am not a person of faith.

Another time, I was employed in a medical facility where patients socialized in a large open area. Patients could also hear the conversations of the staff very well. A coworker who I supervised at the time, who also worked at the local hospital, began telling a story about a trans person that had come into the ER. This nurse, nearly shouting, told this patient's story in great detail to myself and several other staff. This is a professional taboo as a nurse. Sharing patient information in such a way is actually illegal in this country. Nevertheless, they illustrated the whole story: how the patient came into the ER and had been seen by the prescriber, and when it was time for the nurse to give the patient their printed prescription they called out the wrong name into the lobby. The trans patient came to the door for their prescription and gave the nurse an earful about using the wrong name and pronouns. The nurse replied with, "Well, this must not be your prescription, then!" And shut the door on the trans person, denying them their prescription. They laughed. They saw this as them winning some kind of logic game over the transgender person.

As their supervisor, I took her aside to educate her about her responsibility with regards to patient privacy and the inappropriateness of denying care to a patient, not to mention bragging about it in front of others. She was obstinate that she had done nothing wrong. She consented to a meeting with our medical director about it. Our medical director agreed with her; she also "saw nothing wrong" with the situation or the nurse's behavior. A month later, this nurse stated that she could no longer work with me due to how uncomfortable *she* felt about this incident. We went to HR together where I was told by HR that I was "too focused on the transgender aspect" of the situation, even though I had not made mention of it since. I was let go the following week.

To me, this all seems like very concrete evidence that I was let go because I spoke up in defence of the dignity and privacy of the transgender patient initially. I filed a complaint with the Department of Fair Housing and Employment in California. But they stated that nothing was wrong with what was done to me since I was still in my probationary period.

You might ask why someone would want to work for a company with such prevailing homophobia and transphobia at the top? The reality is that good jobs are limited in my rural area. You might have similar constraints. Ultimately, where you work, who you work for, and when and how you speak up at work is going to be something that each person considers very carefully.

Sometimes it's scary to make waves, especially when it comes to our careers. But what about trans people and their careers? If you silently hide behind the protections and privileges you have passing as a cisgender and heterosexual person, you are perpetuating the culture of inequality and doing nothing for your visibly queer friends.

As a thought experiment, take an inventory of the professional consequences you imagine you may or may not encounter at work if you do speak up about LGBTQ rights and justice. Could you envision:

- Losing your job?

- Alienating a paying client?

- Losing camaraderie with a group of coworkers?

- Upsetting your boss?

- Getting moved to a different department?

- Having your current power and scope restricted or constricted?

- Being made fun of or getting ridiculed?

What is a tolerable risk to you? Everyone will have their own answer to this question. Lately, I'm heartened by several books that I've seen coming out by whistleblowers that detail their experiences—what they've lost, and what they've gained. A favorite is Steve Magness' *Win the Inside Game* from 2025. It talks in detail about investigating one's own values and what it costs to stand up for them.

Next, I'll talk about some different types of workplaces and scenarios you might find yourself in, and ways to envision yourself making a positive difference where you are.

Working in an Inclusive Workplace

Do you work in a place that is explicitly affirming? With rainbow flags on doors and in cubicles? Do you have DEI groups promoted by HR, like an LGBTQ affinity group or Pride committee? Does your company march in the local Pride parade or have a table at Pride events?

If the above is all true, great. As you instinctively know, you will likely be protected if you speak up on behalf of queer and trans coworkers in this setting. That is quite a privilege.

You may think that because you work for such a place, there is no need for you to speak up. But that may not be true. LGBTQ acceptance at work is truly a spectrum, and might have a moving goalpost—the situation may be fluid.

You may be in a situation where there is a person in HR or on the executive team who is passionate about LGBTQ justice, and so did the work to get rainbow stickers put up in places. But this does not mean that all staff have attended LGBTQ cultural sensitivity training or feel comfortable speaking with LGBTQ clients or have any knowledge about queer justice. You may have discriminatory policies in place regarding queer couples' benefits or healthcare for transgender people, and most people wouldn't even know.

Then, what if that one HR or leadership person leaves the company? This could put the organization back at step one. And worse, the rainbow stickers that remain could give people a false sense that the organization has done queer justice work, or indeed, cares about it at all.

Rainbow flags stick out. I've been in situations where people generally believe that they work in a kind and inclusive environment because there was one cubicle with a rainbow flag. But the reality was that only one person—the person with the flag—felt comfortable talking to queer clients. So everyone sent all the queer clients to that one person, and thus were able to avoid talking to queer clients themselves. Furthermore, their avoidance perpetuated the idea that it is difficult, awkward, or scary to serve queer clients.

A workplace that fully practices queer justice looks like queer people at work who are not afraid to be themselves, to look and act differently, and to talk about their personal lives. It looks like a staff who are not afraid of or intimidated by interacting with queer clients. It is a workplace where queer justice is talked about openly, without people bowing out or silencing the conversation because they are afraid it might be controversial.

Our lives and rights are not controversial. We have the right to be ourselves. Justice is not controversial. Everyone should be interested in justice. Paint it that way.

So, if you work in an inclusive and protective workplace, you still likely have ways you can make a difference. What kind of power do you have to make change and implement programs where you are? Can you be the person who:

- Lobbies for gender-neutral restroom signage?

- Creates an internal LGBTQ affinity or Pride group?

- Connects with queer coworkers to find out what they want or need?

- Encourages or organizes participation in local Pride events?

- Creates partnerships with local LGBTQ organizations?

- Starts a tradition of volunteering with local LGBTQ-serving organizations?

- Introduces LGBTQ sensitivity training (provided by local queer professionals)?

LGBTQ Welcoming Workplace Principles

Something a next-level ally can do if they feel they have a pretty safe work environment is to investigate how inviting and welcoming your workplace is to incoming queers at a structural level. Does your company actively recruit queers? If not, why not?

Some features of a workplace that is not only safe, but welcoming are:

- Standardized parental leave policies not based on gender, marriage status, or role as a parent.

- Ability to add domestic partners to insurance policies.

- Insurance policies that cover transgender surgeries (most do, but not all!)

- Recruitment activities at local LGBTQ job fairs.

- LGBTQ affinity groups or internal networking groups.

- "Take Your Child to Work Day" or "Bring Your Spouse to Work Day" rather than gendered events like "Dad/Daughter Day" or "Bring Your Wife to Work Day."

- Internal Pride celebrations.

- Recognition of Pride month and LGBTQ history or news items in the company newsletter.

- An informational sheet or webpage letting potential recruits know about these inclusive policies and the company's commitment to creating an LGBTQ welcoming workplace.

Ask your HR department how they are doing compared to this list. Challenge them to tick off each item. Offer to help make that happen.

Working in a Hostile Workplace

If you have a workplace where you hear hateful things about minority groups, your organization has a religious affiliation, or you are just generally afraid of speaking up for any number of reasons—past, present, or future—you have some thinking and searching to do before you can implement the ideas in the previous section.

First, do you have a trusted friend at work? Someone you can bounce these concepts and ideas off of? A person like this can be a crucial resource. Second, think about minimizing your risk. This means thinking hard about the most strategic way to make an impact at the place you work, and in the most defensible way possible. There are lots of ways I have done this kind of work because I have worked in primarily hostile places throughout my life. Working in healthcare is generally not warm and fuzzy. It's a bit cutthroat. And the nursing profession in particular is among the most traditional and conservative of professions, very late to the game in allowing people who dress differently into their ranks, and focused on old-fashioned and formal ways of greeting and interacting with people. It's a weird place. I've also had practice with hostile school administrators with whom I've been hired to collaborate after some terrible incident happened on their campus.

Because of these experiences, I've come up with and practiced a wide variety of tactics for hostile situations. (I haven't gotten fired from *all* my jobs, and I'm still working right now, to be clear.) Most of my tactics for doing advocacy work with hostile audiences fall into one or more of the following categories, which I will explain in more detail below:

- Killing them with kindness.

- Illustrating the issue as a civil rights issue by drawing parallels to other minority groups.

- Pointing out legal transgressions.

- Co-opting company language.

KILLING THEM WITH KINDNESS

"Killing them with kindness" works so well, in so many situations—even outside of the workplace. I highly recommend thinking of this as the main knife in your multi-tool. Keep it sharp.

I think of it as the mindset of an aggressively enthusiastic helper. Like, "Hey, guys! I just learned this *incredible fact . . .*" or "*Actually,* studies show . . . [insert helpful information here]."

It's an attitude. Some people are better at this than others. Honestly, I'm not super great at it, and default instead to sarcasm and passive-aggression way too often. That's not necessarily what we are going for. Ideally, what we want to communicate is a *genuine love for all people,* right? So, own that, feel that.

It takes practice to get this to feel natural. But it's worth it.

Using this skill in the context of justice at work requires confidence and pre-existing knowledge about issues queer employees or clients may run into at your workplace. Once you know what these issues are, you can frame those concerns and hypothetical scenarios in a universally loving and caring way. Killing them with kindness can be about building the conversation about universal values, rights, and ideals, but then skillfully and quickly, as an aside almost, reminding people that queer people fall into the category of "all people," too. Done right, this can be impossible to argue with. Killing them with kindness can also mean being overly cheerful while offering advice or perspective on an issue.

Example: Coworkers are complaining about management marking two single room restrooms that had been previously marked male and female as gender-neutral. Maybe coworkers are complaining that now men will make both of them gross. You could drop in and helpfully offer, "*Actually,* I've noticed that in other places, this seems to have shamed men into being more tidy! And neither restroom gets especially filthy anymore."

Maybe they are complaining that it will now be confusing and lead to awkward encounters. You could cheerily interject, "*Actually,* since now no one has to remember which is which, over time it will become totally natural to notice all people coming out of either one, just like the restrooms in your house! Simple!"

In these examples, the subtext of the complaints imply that trans and non-binary people are a source of unnecessary confusion, so you didn't even need to mention them by name. All you needed to do was point out that it isn't actually a hardship to have gender-neutral restrooms in the workplace.

Here is another example, this one offers a way to slip the issue of queer justice in while making a broader point about universal rights. Say a coworker is complaining about having to change the name and gender on someone's school record, medical record, credit card, library card, etc. You could slip in and remind them that, "*Actually,* everyone has the right to change their name at any time in this country, like when they get married or divorced, or even if they just want to. This includes LGBTQ people. Also we see clerical errors made all the time that we have to correct and this is no different, really. It is *super easy,* let me show you how!"

Drawing Parallels with Other Civil Rights Struggles

Different minority groups *do not* face the same inequalities or barriers and in general cannot be lumped together. But in this very specific situation—communicating with hostile people you are working alongside—it can be an effective tool. Think of it more as a *banding together* for mutual protection and solidarity.

Example: Someone is insinuating that same sex couples should not be allowed to marry, be put on the insurance of their partner, etc. Remind them that the right to marry was not available to all people for most of this country's history. Most states had laws prohibiting Black and Native American people from marrying white people (anti-miscegenation laws) and preventing Chinese people from immigrating and marrying. This was foundationally racist, as it prevented these groups from owning property, inheriting property, and creating generational wealth. That's why marriage equality is crucial for all people, and why we can't single any one group out.

"Just a helpful historical fact!"

Pointing Out Legal Transgressions

Identifying any legal infractions that your agency may be guilty of is a very direct and efficient way to effect change at an organization.

There are plenty of instances where it is *not* safe to be a whistleblower. I have definitely been retaliated against for speaking out about HIPAA (medical privacy) violations, as I described earlier, and for pointing out Medicare fraud. I personally don't regret these decisions. I feel safe and secure enough in my career now that I can also freely admit that I did these things in the past, and I know that I never want to work for an agency that retaliates against whistleblowers ever again. That's my choice, position, and privilege. Your mileage may vary. Not everyone is in this position, not everyone has the freedom to speak up in this directly challenging way.

At the same time, there are instances where pointing out legal transgressions can be the safest *and* most effective course of action. I suggest you carefully analyze each unique situation, bounce it off coworkers if you are able, and develop a bullet-proof stance before attempting this.

An example of where this has worked for me is when I discovered that California made it a legal requirement for certain large healthcare agencies to collect gender and sexuality data from patients. Collecting this data is crucial for research regarding the health disparities that LGBTQ people face. However, in practice, this data is seldom gathered. Many people don't fill out forms completely and sometimes staff people are too nervous to ask the questions. So, the data doesn't get captured. The state of California actually did an audit of the situation a few years after the law passed that affirmed, yep, hardly anyone is collecting sexuality and gender identity data.

After I confirmed that this was true with the other department heads in my organization, I decided to point out to my bosses that we, like most other agencies, were doing a poor job of collecting this data. They actually responded super positively, thanked me for pointing this out, and started to take steps to get staff better educated on how to collect this data.

In educational settings, I've noticed that I get immediate traction if I make sure to helpfully remind administrators that an exclusionary or unjust practice "is a civil rights issue." That is language that perks up their ears; its language they understand. It alerts them to a potential legal infraction (discriminating against or failing to protect the safety of kids, for instance), and it also blends into our next strategy of co-opting company jargon.

CO-OPTING COMPANY LANGUAGE

Using people's language against them is one of my absolute favorite tactics.

What kind of rah-rah language does your company prefer? What kind of values do they claim to be passionate about? What kind of jargon do they perk up to and understand instinctively? Co-opt that language, and use it when you talk about queer justice and equality.

Is your company basically only about the dollars? Plenty of research exists about the fact that many gay couples are childless and therefore have more disposable income than other families. There is no question that we have spending power and are a market to court. A quick internet search for marketing research on the subject finds that we have billions in purchasing power, and often outspend straight folks on luxury items like travel, entertainment, and cosmetics.[13] Bring this up to them when they are marketing or developing a new product, it might encourage them to keep queer experience and people in mind.

Basically, lean into whatever your company already purports to value, be that reputation enhancement through aligning with causes young people find important, exploring untapped markets, or increasing brand loyalty though partnerships with trusted LGBTQ voices. If nothing else, having these conversations can be a good litmus test of what the values of your workplace really are.

In the end, there may not be much that you feel safe doing or

---

13 "LGBT Market Research," SIS International Research, https://www.sisinternational.com/expertise/industries/lgbt-market-research/.

speaking up about if you work in a hostile environment. In that case, it is still good and useful work to insert queer concepts and ideas into everyday conversations in the lunchroom. Just being overheard using caring and inclusive language, in a place where none exists, can be a powerful start to changing the culture of a workplace. This work takes years, and you personally may never see any tangible result. But you just may have been the person to start to turn the tide.

Speaking Up Online

Speaking up and speaking out about trans rights and queer issues on your social media might feel daunting. What expertise do you have on the subject? Why would anyone want to hear what you have to say as a straight person?

The fact is that queer and trans rights are human rights, and talking about it needs to get destigmatized. We do this by sharing about it, and thereby normalizing it. This is work for everyone, not just queer and trans people. You will find this gets easier with practice and that you will eventually craft your own voice on the subject. There are many different hats you might choose to wear online based on your own interests, strengths, industry, or location. Some of them include:

- Sharer of queer and trans made content.

- Explainer of laws and news items.

- Applauder of queer and trans celebrities, icons, and advocates.

- Promoter of local Pride activities and resources.

- Chronicler of your personal journey towards a more holistic allyship.

The chart below offers specific ideas about how to be a next-level ally online.

DIFFERENT WAYS TO SHARE LGBTQ CONTENT ONLINE

ACTION	EXAMPLES
Sharing Queer-Made Content	Are you a media or culture enthusiast? Can you: • Be intentional about seeking out and sharing content by queer artists? • Cheer on queer storylines featured in media you are currently watching? • Advocate for queer authors for your book club? • Follow, comment on, and share discussions led by queer celebrities and voices?
Explaining LGBTQ-Focused News	Are you a news junkie? Do you work in law or government? Will you: • Use your social media, blog, or other platform to explain how LGBTQ-focused news and legislation might affect those in your immediate community? • Be intentional about following and commenting on the actions of the Supreme Court that affect queer people?

Promoting Local Pride and Advocacy Groups	Does your city or town have a vibrant local queer culture? Can you: • Share information about local queer events and meetups? • Profile the work advocates are doing in your area?
Aligning with Queer-Owned Local Business	Do you love to go out to eat? Patronize local shops? How about: • Profiling and promoting local queer-owned businesses? • Creating cross promotional and co-branding opportunities?
Chronicling Your Journey Towards Better Allyship	Do you want to inspire other people in your online communities to become better allies? You could: • Share about your personal growth and learning journey with regards to queer justice. • Share articles and resources you have read. • Describe books you are reading. • Explain things as you learn them in real-time. • Be transparent about blind spots you have identified or things you are finding difficult or challenging like learning to use they/them pronouns. • Share difficulties with a spirit of openness and encouragement and invite others to take up the challenge with you.

Once you start opening these kinds of conversations online, you never know where the discussion might go. If talking about queer culture online is new for you and those who follow you, responses from close friends might surprise you the most.

Model the Right Language

So, conversation is important, to say the least. But so much online conversation veers toward the negative quickly, and it is frustrating. What to do? As I said before, a great way to address negativity is the kill them with kindness approach. If you see a phobic or hateful comment on the internet, comment right back about how everyone deserves equal rights and respect. Do not mimic or mock any of their hateful language. Just answer back with the correct and respectful language. This is educational in itself, if not for the commenter directly, for people watching silently who might be neutral or on the fence about the situation. By answering back in simple and inclusive language, we educate on how to dialogue respectfully.

You might think that staying silent is neutral. But it is not. Not responding to a hateful comment is perpetuating the culture of hate and silence.

Calling Out Hypersexualization

Conservative crusaders attack us by sexualizing every conversation and topic. They try to paint drag story time as something sexual. In negative political messaging they use us as examples of disgusting, provocative, and perverse things to be afraid of.

We need you to step in and politely remind them that LGBTQ identities are not about just sex. They are about love and relationships. Family. Kids. Getting older. Everything human. To reduce us to sex acts is a hateful tactic meant to strip us of our humanity. This needs pointing out.

Explain to people that talking about gender and sexuality doesn't necessarily mean talking about sex acts. I'd go further and argue that talking about queer justice doesn't mean a conversation about sex at all: it's about jobs, equal pay, equal right to play sports, to marry and have access to the social and financial protections offered to heterosexual couples, and to the simple right to dress how one wants and be called by the correct name.

Support Local Orgs with Likes and Comments

Even something as small as "liking" and sharing LGBTQ-focused events or venues on socials is helpful. When you do this, you are legitimizing the people who are putting on the events and increasing the visibility of the event so that more queer people become aware of it. Liking and following queer and trans justice nonprofits is useful for these reasons, but also so that you become aware of local events in your area, which is something really important I'll talk about in later chapters.

Speaking Out Everywhere

Speaking up online can mean speaking up in comment spaces that veer into homophobia or transphobia. Because if those kinds of comments are let lie, queer and trans people see that as a signal that it is an unsafe community to speak up in, leading them to feel and thus stay doubly alienated from the social conversation. We have to make it so that trans and queer people feel comfortable being visible on all platforms. This is equality—and it will also just so happen to lead to even greater understanding and empathy. It's a positive, building circle.

These strategies work on the internet, but also work in real time. Beginning to call out homophobia or transphobia at home or at work, online and even in public spaces, is an essential next step to take in creating our culture of acceptance. Sometimes, it is hard to envision the ripple effect we might have. But if there is one thing I have seen, it is that people are routinely capable of making ripples that end up surprising even themselves.

If you don't think that talking and empathy building are effective tools for change, think about twenty years ago. Do you think there was more visibility, rights, and justice for trans people then or less? If there were fewer rights then and less care available, what happened? People spoke up!

CHAPTER 6

CELEBRATE

A next-level ally doesn't just subtract and correct. They add. In this chapter, I will show you a whole bunch of different ways that you can add celebration of your queer friends and their unique milestones to your yearly calendar. Things like coming out parties, pet birthdays, sober birthdays, and other cute ideas to inspire your creativity.

Queerness is not something we have to hide anymore. Increasingly, people are recognizing new and different ways to celebrate our queerness and lives.

Proud to Be Queer

Think about it: what is pride? Pride is the opposite of shame. Shame, fear, hiding, and secrecy were the hallmarks of queerness in the 1950s and before, according to pretty much all of the accounts in *The Stonewall Reader*, a wonderful book edited by the New York Public Library. Secret societies and underground bars were the ways queer people connected back then because you could get fired from your job, kicked out of the army, or even go to jail if you came out (or were forced out by being discovered by the wrong person).

Pride celebrations were established to turn this narrative around, and stomp it out.

Now, we are able to show we are proud of who we are, and who we love. Thing is, the way society is laid out still does not give us as many chances to celebrate milestones as straight people do. Many of us are unmarried and childless. We never got a honeymoon. Engagement party. Stag party. Bridal shower. Baby shower. Multiple baby showers. *Everyone* at work pitches in for a buffet, party, and gifts for an expecting mom. I get it—kids are expensive. But at the same time, this is not something I'll ever experience. It begins to feel like the cisheteronormative world is just something we observe from afar, while the real, queer world is still hidden from view. Or, visible only to a select few.

Happily, queer weddings are legal in the United States, for now. So we have that, and it goes without saying that this is a huge thing to celebrate—something that has only relatively recently even become legal.

Celebrate the fuck out of queer couples you know getting married. If they are OK with it, share the heck out of pictures of the event. This normalizes the event for the people on your feed who have never seen such a thing. For lots of people, queerness is still a foreign thing, shrouded in mystery. Part of being a next-level ally is drawing back the curtain, and making us human again.

Milestones for Queer Adults

Do you have sad queer people in your life? I do. Queer people are disproportionately affected by depression and anxiety, sometimes the result of feeling left out by life, unseen, unnoticed, uncelebrated. Are there events they might have missed out on? Think about what is important to them. Maybe it's not something we traditionally celebrate. But, could it be?

GRADUATIONS LATER IN LIFE

Some of us have taken a longer or winding path in our careers. Some of us were discouraged from doing things we wanted to do earlier in life because of gender expectations. As a result, many of us find new careers, new sports, new interests later in life. Also, some of us had extremely poor and unaffirming high school experiences. We may have opted out of prom and graduation or participated and had a terrible experience.

We don't always celebrate graduations as adults. Many have no desire to. Definitely respect that, if so! But maybe your adult queer friend has been quietly exploring classes or has earned themselves a shiny, new degree at a later age? Maybe a graduation party would feel like an affirming do-over for a terrible high school experience. Or maybe, they are just due for a celebration! Ask if they would like you to make that happen for them.

SOBER BIRTHDAYS

Many in sober communities celebrate the day they committed to a sober life as their "sober birthday." Can you offer a way to help make this a big event? Or suggest they have one if they haven't ever had one? Throw them one, if they show an interest?

HONEYMOONS

Suggest a honeymoon to your unmarried, queer couple friends who don't have any plans to marry. Queer couples can choose to opt out of marriage for a ton of reasons. Maybe one partner doesn't have an accepting family. Maybe it's too expensive and logistical, and they see it as only a thing for straight people. Maybe they just see no reason to.

But they still deserve to celebrate the committed relationship they have! Point this out. And if you are their boss, can you be extra kind about helping them take time off work the same way you would for a married couple?

Pet Adoptions

All people, gay or straight, can feel like their pets are their children and give them the same attention and investment. Do you think your queer friends would like to have a celebration for the new pet addition to their family? Kind of like a baby shower? Ask them! Make it happen if they love the idea.

Coming Out Party

I have never personally been to one or heard of one happening around me, but I think the idea of a coming out party sounds just wonderful. Pretty much all the dollar stores around me seem to have rainbow and unicorn-themed party favors and decorations year-round now. This might be a California thing. Regardless, throwing a coming out party for the new queer person in your life sounds like an easy thing to do.

It could look like anything. It doesn't matter what age they are; it doesn't matter if they came out years ago. Ask them if they would like to celebrate the event! Many people will have a date in their memory for when they first decided to tell the greater world that they are queer or trans. This takes massive courage, which likely took years to develop. Ask them if they would like to share the story with you, and celebrate it!

It's a Boy/Girl Parties for Trans Adults

Have a binary trans friend? (A binary transgender person does not identify as non-binary.) Did they ever have a coming out party? Would they like one? Transitioning one's gender is a fuck ton of work and effort, and most lose some amount of family and friends along the way. It can be a huge sacrifice. And it is not yet celebrated in our society.

Would they like you to go to the dollar store, get a bunch of "It's a Boy/Girl" decorations and paraphernalia, and throw them the proper baby shower they never had? How about your non-binary friend? Would they like a party themed with "It's NOT a Boy?"

Get creative.

Aggressively Gender Trans Friends

As I alluded to before, it can feel so good to be aggressively, affirmingly gendered by friends. Just that can feel like a form of celebration. Every trans person will have their own comfort level with this. But as a rule, it is generally a very nice thing to do, for example, to compliment a trans woman's outfit, hairstyle, makeup, or anything else she has put effort and love into in order to feel her way through her gender, and present in a way that makes her feel ecstatic.

And it's pretty much always a good call to invite her to ladies' night.

For me, I am a transgender guy, so when I came out, friends had only yet known me as a woman. Looking at me through the lens of masculinity was something new. I watched as men had a visually obvious process as they realized, paused, and then put into practice different ways of hugging me, shaking my hand, and speaking with me within a group of other men. It's different.

I will always remember one friend who immediately understood this and gave a very sporty and manly thump and slap to my (well healed!) new chest the first time seeing me after chest surgery.

I want to share another story I tell people all the time. I live in a fairly rural and small community. To the north are even smaller and more rural communities where lots of folks enjoy guns, fishing, and such. I have a good friend who was living up there at the time. The day I came up to visit and come out to him as trans, I was nervous. I wasn't afraid he would decide to ultimately hate me and end the friendship, but at the same time, I wondered if this would make our friendship awkward or uncomfortable in some way. I wondered if it would change our friendship.

I told him I was trans, and that I would be transitioning to living my life as a man from then on. There was a pause as the lightbulb flickered on, I could see it. It only took a few seconds. And in those seconds, he intuitively figured out *exactly* how our relationship would change—for the more affirming and the better. Without further questions or preamble about the transition process, he said, "Okay. Do you want to go ride around in the car real fast and shoot guns later?"

I said yes, yes I would very much like to do those things.

This isn't to say that all trans people want to fall into stereotypical, normative boxes of masculinity or femininity, or that they instantly need to play football or go to the salon. Far from it. Some actively reject all that. But with this friend, in this time, place, circumstance, and in our life experiences up until this point, this was the most affirming thing he could come to off the cuff. And personally, *I loved it.*

Some folks will *love* for you to invite them to the nail salon or spa. Or the baseball game. The stag party. Some won't. Everyone will be different. But I think if there is a general rule, it is to think about your queer and trans friends in the exact same way as the other people in your life, and don't let assumptions *get in the way* of inviting them to things. The worst thing to do would be to overthink it and *not invite them* to *any* gendered things. Some folks might appreciate it if you are a bit extra about inviting them and making sure they feel welcome and included in their newfound place in the world.

Directly *asking* your non-binary friends if they would like to join you in traditionally gendered activities, rather than guessing or assuming or, by default, excluding them, is a great way to get to know their personal preferences and outlook on life in general in a deeper and more meaningful way. Do that.

Teaching Your Friends Gender Stuff

When I started living as a man, for at least the first two years, it felt like a continual discovery of things I didn't know how to do. How do I order a haircut in a masculine-type barbershop? How do I shave my face? How do I form sentences and enunciate in a masculine way? It's a thing I only started to notice after I transitioned. I started to hear things and say, "Wow, that sounds kind of girly." It took a lot of mental processing and community help to figure out exactly why that was and then put it into practice. Also, how do I hug a man, as a man? How do I do the complicated handshake-fist bump things? (I'm still working on this one.)

For binary trans women, there can be the same learning curve. How to put on different kinds of bras? How should they look and feel? How to choose and apply makeup? How to ask for what you want at the nail shop?

Offer to accompany your trans and queer friends into these gendered spaces, and offer the language and norms they may or may not know. Figure out what makes each unique person *feel affirmed.*

Do you *own* a nail salon, barbershop, alterations business, hat shop, lingerie shop, shoe shop, or some other kind of business that historically has been heavily gendered? Could you offer discounts, incentives, or promotions that reach out to LGBTQ people directly? This could go a long way to helping people feel affirmed in a non-judgmental way. Could it be a whole advertising campaign for you? In partnership with your local Pride center? You could reach out to your local LGBTQ organizations to ask what they need that you may be able to offer.

How about holding a short seminar about how to order a haircut or do makeup at your local LGBTQ center? It could be a win-win; you're promoting your business and building community ties. Maybe your business has a podcast or video-based social media presence. Could you have an episode or short where you interview a queer or trans client about their first experiences either with your business or your industry in general? Lots of people would find this interesting, not just queer people. You could be training next-generation allies.

Being out and visible as queer and trans can have consequences that take a mental, physical, and financial toll. Sometimes, the work we do to assert ourselves and stay alive leads us to miss out on some milestones that we watch others around us celebrating. As a creative friend, you can help us find alternate ways to celebrate and make sure we feel included and welcomed in spaces that are new to us.

Chapter 7

CREATE VISIBILITY

Creating visibility for LGBTQ people can happen anywhere within your sphere of influence. This will look different for everybody. You can think of creating visibility as a philosophy that starts to draw together everything we have been learning so far. In fact, many of the suggestions in this book for lending a hand to or supporting your LGBTQ community create visibility as a side effect.

For example, liberating restrooms from the gender binary is a visible effect that people in the immediate area will notice. Many will see it as a nod towards the LGBTQ community. Some will see this as a positive, some might use it as a point of contention. Therefore, you can see how through the process of creating visibility, we are shining a light onto existing problems and inequities, which might make people uncomfortable. We are creating talking points that we may have to defend. This is why we needed to start the book with a few chapters that armed you with counters to common attacks on LGBTQ people and language about justice. You will need all of it once you start creating visibility at home, at work, or in the classroom.

Virtue Signaling

Some hand-wringing has been done in the last few years about a concept called "virtue signaling." The foul of virtue signaling can be called when someone is perceived to be doing a lot of talking about justice in order to gain social capital, to look cool, to sound smart. I feel like this is akin to the narrative of hateful groups who accuse LGBTQ teens of taking on queer identities as a disposable fashion trend.

A more nuanced look at the idea separates talk from action. It is now argued that virtue signaling is a label for those who talk without action. When I think of signaling, I think of someone waving a big flag, going "Look at me and how cool I am!" As allies, we obviously want to avoid this, and make sure any attention we are drawing is to the issues, to justice, and to uplifting queer voices as opposed to our own. And hopefully it goes without saying that we need to *do* things, not just talk. I think the majority of people buying this book will automatically agree with this, it's what we're all here learning to do.

So, if you take action and you are doing everything you can to make sure that the narrative stays on the facts of queer justice and uplifts queer voices higher than your own (if you are straight and cis), you can point this out to people who might accuse you of virtue signaling.

Pinkwashing

Greenwashing is the corporate practice of using marketing that appears to trumpet environmental justice, think green or brown colored packaging with pictures of trees, when in reality, their company isn't doing much for the environment at all. It's not using recycled products where it can, not reducing water consumption, or maybe it's even actively harming the environment.

Same with pinkwashing. When a company is accused of pinkwashing, people are accusing them of marketing towards queer people while behind the scenes the company has a conservative agenda, supports hateful representatives or legislation, or is generally oppressive to people in some fashion.

Take care to not engage in pinkwashing. As stated, I think that in most cases this boils down to a retail company that markets products towards queer people, but engages in conservative politics on the side. It is unlikely that you have influence in both of these areas simultaneously, unless you are a CEO or board member. But what you may be able to do is point out pinkwashing if you see it happening. Refer back to "Chapter Five: Speaking Up at Work and Online." Consider this another concept to tuck away in your mental filing cabinet for if and when it comes up.

And don't let people accuse you of pinkwashing if you are, in fact, doing queer justice work at the same time as marketing towards queers or uplifting queer voices and visibility.

Stickers and Flags

Hey, did you know that it's OK to wear rainbows as a straight person? That it can be a conversation starter, giving you the chance to explain that you are a strong ally of all queer people?

It's also OK for you to have a rainbow sticker or flag in your cubicle. But do some work on articulating what it means to you, and be prepared with thoughtful replies to questions about it. Share what you have learned about queer justice, and justice in general. Use it to signal your support for or against local actions or legislation in your area.

A rainbow sticker on the door of a retail store, restaurant, or medical clinic signals to me that the staff, at least for the most part, are not going to be rude or disgusted if I engage in queer public displays of affection (PDA), are going to respect my pronouns, and won't bat an eye if I am a man wearing a skirt.

If you are considering rainbow stickers or flags at the entry to your establishment, can you make these claims? If so, *please do* put stickers and flags up. They are comforting to see. We do look for them, and to me, they often make a difference whether I stop in a shop in an area I'm newly exploring or whether I breeze on by. They are meaningful to me.

I'm not sure exactly what this illustrates, but I feel compelled to share the story of the first medical clinic where I received trans care. There was no trans care available where I was (rural California in 2016), so I had actually moved 150 miles and gotten a new job to be able to get care at this particular clinic. It was the most accessible clinic for me, and had taken a lot of asking around and word-of-mouth to find. When I got there, I found a small and drab building made of concrete, mostly hidden from street view by vegetation. There was no rainbow flag on the door (much less a trans flag). When I approached the counter, I gave them my new, masculine name (Eli), and said I had made an appointment.

They sneered in confusion, asking, "*What* did you say your name was?" I *definitely* had given my new name, Eli, when I made an appointment. I remember it being a new experience and a bit nerve-wracking. They were asking for my deadname. (Trans people use the term "deadname" for their name[s], now changed, that they were assigned at birth.) Since my deadname was feminine, it was now apparent to all the patients waiting in the lobby and any staff within earshot that I was trans. As a baby trans person, I felt very uncomfortable. I wondered to myself, even though I had done my research on this clinic, "Am I even in the right place?"

Perhaps it was appropriate that they didn't have a rainbow flag up; forcing me to out myself meant their cultural sensitivity was very low. But at the same time, a flag would have given me some sense that I was in the right place—that there *was* trans care to be found there. As it was, I sat in the lobby, not exactly sure if I was going to see a doctor who was going to help or understand me, at all.

There may not be an easy answer here. I know that rainbow stickers give me a sense of security. I know that people warn us against creating a *false sense* of security. I also know that stickers and flags create conversation and can be used by management or administration to *signal* a culture shift within an organization.

Sometimes, the act of simply starting the conversation about putting up flags or stickers can be very illuminating. You may be surprised at the enthusiasm, or resistance, you might meet. This is valuable information that will help you build your strategies and find partners in your justice work.

Pins and Posters

Putting your pronouns on a pin or your name badge (or email signature) signals to non-binary people that you understand they/them pronouns, and can encourage them to share theirs with you. Which is the first step towards building trust with them!

I've seen some institutions give out rainbow pins with a small card, asking the wearer to make a pledge to complete an online educational module about LGBTQ equality. If you are an educator, you can order and download affirming and educational posters from GLSEN (more about GLSEN in Chapter 11). Search to see if you have a local chapter. Also check out teacherspayteachers.com for printable posters and activities you can buy for a nominal fee.

Health professionals can find LGBTQ messaging from the California State Department of Public Health on a variety of topics. Also, the LGBTQIA+ Health Education Center from the Fenway Institute has a variety of posters reaching out to LGBTQ clients filed under Patient Education Materials.

Like stickers, posters and pins can create a similar welcoming effect.

Elevate and Advertise

Has your organization used queer and trans models in its advertising and outreach activities? If not, why not? How can you advocate for this? It is important to see queer and trans faces in marketing and outreach materials. The "why" is part of a larger, cultural question which might be outside the scope of this book. But think about how our media landscape prizes skinny bodies and pale faces and the result of that: devaluing bodies that aren't like that, especially those that are bigger and non-white (i.e., most people's bodies). And think about the lifetimes upon lifetimes of work that have been devoted to dismantling that.

If you try to look at this through the queer lens, you might begin to understand what growing up in this media hellscape is for queer people. Growing up, I never saw queer people kiss in movies. What I heard instead was grown-ups and peers talking about how queerness is disgusting. My young mind internalized this as true, and the lack of queer representation in the media seemed to confirm that queerness was disgusting, taboo, and off-limits.

I also never saw a trans man in the media (or anywhere that I was aware of) until I was in my early thirties. So, I never knew that transitioning was possible for me. Seeing queer folks represented in media of all kinds, even something as transient as an advertisement, can have the most incredibly profound effects on people's lives. This doesn't just go for major motion pictures or TV series. Just seeing queer folks holding hands in the health insurance commercial honestly helps chip away at the prevailing narrative. The narrative I grew up with is that queer people don't get married, don't get the princess, aren't part of the sports team, aren't considered in healthcare, don't belong at the party, and just plain don't matter.

So, depending on your work and roles in the community, you might be able to create queer visibility through elevating and advertising. Ask yourself these questions:

- Do you have opportunities to sponsor a local LGBTQ-led organization or Pride celebration?

    a. Can you co-brand with them on their website and socials?

    b. Can you elevate their voices, expand their reach, and normalize their activities in your community?

- Do you work for or own a media publication, newspaper, magazine, podcast, or YouTube channel?

    a. Have you considered inviting local queer leaders as speaking guests?

- Have you solicited or partnered with LGBTQ organizations to find local talent for your craft fair?

- How have you advocated for queer and trans representation, celebration, and elevation in your sphere of influence?

Demand Neutral Bathrooms

California and Vermont have laws that state that all single-occupancy public restrooms are to be marked gender-neutral. And why not? Isn't the toilet in your house gender-neutral?

I have a secret hope that the gradual making of all bathrooms into gender-neutral places will eventually shame men into being more tidy. But that aside, gender-neutral restrooms are important for your trans friends. Especially early in transition, bathrooms are an extremely scary place to be. Going into public restrooms of the opposite gender to the ones you've been using for your entire life is a terrifying prospect for most people. Many people create elaborate strategies to avoid it, for a long time.

Imagine walking into a place where you might face heightened scrutiny, hostility, and, at worst, violence. And imagine doing it while you have to pee really bad. And while you are already living in a private hell of anxiety about your appearance to the world. Try to imagine all these things at once.

Neutral restrooms can go a long way towards alleviating this. It can be such a relief to turn the corner and discover a neutral restroom. Not only does that signal that this is an inclusive and hate-free establishment. It also removes the internal conversation about how to look and act in a space that we were not raised and socialized in. Expectations can be so tiresome!

So, what can you do about this? Whenever you see single-occupancy restrooms that are still gendered, speak to the management about changing it. If you are in the above mentioned states in the United States, it is easy. You can simply alert them to the fact that it is the law. My usual tactic in this situation is to say what I want to say in as few words as possible. This lets the management imagine or assume that you know or are familiar with the apparatus that would enforce said law. Especially if you speak with authority. Simply informing people about the law is a great tactic in general—no further explanation needs to be given.

If you aren't in a state where marking single-occupancy public restrooms as gender-neutral is the law or norm, you can take the time to explain to the proprietors that this practice makes all customers feel welcome here. Again, be brief and use universally kind words (it's hard to argue with *making customers feel welcome*). Hopefully, this plants the notion in their head about why this is a good idea. A receptive ear will continue to consider the "hows" and "whys" on their own later.

If you encounter hostility, ask them why they think this isn't a good idea? Maybe there is a urinal in one and not the other. They think this will confuse people. Tell them that you think people can handle it. I've seen some places mark single room restrooms as "with urinals" and "without." You could suggest this.

Maybe they'll state that they simply don't care. You can simply state back that you DO care, implying that you are happy to take your business elsewhere over this issue. Let them digest that. If they remain obstinate, simply walk away without another word, never to return.

You can do all this while not in the presence of trans friends. You can do this regardless of if you personally have trans friends or even know of any trans people in your town. If you are successful, you will be helping someone. You can be damn sure that there will be a trans person somewhere down the line that will turn the corner and be relieved at the sight of the bathroom that you liberated for them.

Speak Up for Trans Kids

According to Movement Advancement Tracker, twenty U.S. states have laws prohibiting transgender people from using the correct restroom in government buildings and/or K-12 schools in 2026.[14] Clearly, this impacts kids in school the hardest. For me, as an adult, I can choose to not visit or move to these states. But for trans kids in twenty states they are being forced into either the humiliation and bullying that goes along with using the wrong restroom for your gender presentation or delaying their transition until they can get the heck out of the state.

What can you do to support these kids?

I like sharing the story of Mack Beggs, the wrestler from Texas. Mack transitioned from female to male in high school, taking testosterone as a teenager. He developed muscles and wanted to wrestle boys. However, his school board and the various government levels in Texas were all obstinate that he continue to wrestle girls. Why?

There really isn't any logical argument for forcing Mack to wrestle girls. This invariably led to hate and protest against

---

14 "Bans on Transgender People Using Bathrooms and Facilities According to Their Gender Identity," Movement Advancement Project, accessed February 19, 2026, https://www.lgbtmap.org/equality-maps/nondiscrimination/bathroom_bans.

Mack competing, which meant beating pretty much all his competition. The resulting fiasco was illogically used to fuel arguments about the fairness of trans people competing in sports. When, in reality, the most fair thing would have been to simply let Mack wrestle boys like he wanted to.

Did the school administrators *want* Mack to be humiliated and threatened by female competitors and their parents? Did they assume this would just stop him from competing at all? Hard to say. The same lack of logic infects any argument that prevents trans people from using the correct restroom. It is simply a way to attempt to shame kids out of transitioning in the first place, creating the opposite of a "safe space" to be oneself. It creates hostility and division.

If you find people receptive to empathy-creating story sharing, share Mack's story. He gave me permission to do so, years ago.[15]

Normalize Neutral Baby Showers and Announcements

Think about it. Why do we gender infants, anyways? Why is there this huge pink and blue culture to begin with? It serves literally no purpose, and can therefore easily be dismantled. It just takes getting people to think about it.

Hold a neutral baby shower. There are lots of other colors rather than pink and blue. I am seeing showers themed in yellows or purples. These are wonderful colors symbolizing springtime and life. I just saw an announcement with a picture of mom and baby in simple white, together, looking at each other, both in

---

15 For more on Mack's story, watch the 2019 ESPN short made about him called *Mack Wrestles*.

profile. No gender was spoken about. There was no need!

Make a big deal on social media about the shower. You don't have to sit there and explain that it is a neutral baby shower. Just post pictures of your beautiful craftwork that happens to not be pink or blue.

Gender reveal? Just a baby announcement will do, thanks. "It's a _____"? Unnecessary. Why not something with more meaning and heartfelt, like "Welcome, baby!" or "Welcoming our new addition" or "Thankful for family" or simply, "Precious" as a label for a sonogram picture, a picture of a yellow ribbon and pacifier, a picture of a baby. No gender conversation needed.

Educate your friends on why this is not only important, but easy, and *classy*. Regardless of the gender status of their baby, a shower in yellows, greens, teals, purples, earth tones, or just whites and creams is unique, classic, and beautiful in its own right. Be distinctive!

As an older trans person, I have some pictures of myself as a baby and child. But they are locked up in a safe. I don't know why I keep them. Someday certainly, they will end up in the trash. Instead, create a history and legacy that your family can enjoy forever.

Check out Lindz Amer from the show *Queer Kids Stuff* and their book, *Rainbow Parenting: Your Guide to Raising Queer Kids and Their Allies,* for so much more on having and raising kids in an inclusively loving way. They suggest baby showers and bedrooms themed with "under the sea!" Or how about cute forests with cute animals? Birds and rabbits? Or space! Everyone loves space.

Demand Diverse Libraries

Libraries are under attack across the country in various ways. In 2025, it was leaked that our local city officials in Merced, California were considering a proposal to privatize our main county library. This news was met with immediate protest which ended up succeeding in cancelling any further talk about privatization!

Protect your library. Get a library card. Get all the families you know to get a library card. Numbers of users are part of how libraries qualify for funding. You can also support diversity in your library by:

- Asking your local branch to acquire LGBTQ books. Different libraries will have different processes for requesting books. There are lots of "best of" lists that highlight great LGBTQ books and graphic novels published every year. Ask for them specifically.

- Asking if your local library is planning a Pride display and making sure it is front and center. At my local library, the Pride section is literally on the floor, the bottom shelf of a stack, up a flight of stairs, and all the way to the back. It is almost the furthest point from the front door you could possibly choose. This is a question of visibility and representation. Of value.

- Asking about or requesting a Banned Books Week display. Can you offer help in organizing, designing, or promoting one? Banned Books Week is increasingly important as conservative movements around the country seek book bans on all kinds of queer books for readers of all ages. According to PEN America, an organization championing free expression since 1922, book bans since 2021 have risen to levels never before seen.[16] Seeing ourselves reflected in the media is essential to the healthy development of queer identities.

- Starting a book club in partnership with your local library on queer topics. This is even easier now in the age of ebooks and audiobooks which your local library likely can give you access to via apps.

Creating visibility and inclusivity comes in many forms. These are just a few examples to get your creative brain thinking about ways that you can create more invitations for queer folks to feel comfortable and welcome in the spaces you share. Increasing queer visibility and awareness can also have the added effect of forcing heteronormative cis folks to stop and consider why the restroom signage has changed or consider how it makes them feel that queer books have been brought to the center of the room. Do they feel challenged or nervous about it? All of this can start conversations, get people thinking, and give you opportunities to educate people on why a more inclusive world is important and better for everybody.

---

16 "The Normalization of Book Banning," PEN America, October 1, 2025, https://pen.org/report/the-normalization-of-book-banning/.

Chapter 8

SHOW UP

Some people feel like it is important for cis and heteronormative people to show up for queer events. Some don't. Some straight people are concerned that showing up in "someone else's space" might be considered intrusive or rude. And this might be true in some venues. There are queer people who are very protective of certain spaces as queer spaces and are uneasy with a growing straight presence. This is often in the context of gentrifying neighborhoods in which wealthy people drive up prices, eventually displacing marginalized communities of queer people, artists and musicians, and people of color.

I've been known to argue that LGBTQ spaces and groups should include our cis and straight allies in the spirit of embracing radical inclusivity. But not every activist feels this way. In this chapter, I'll discuss different perspectives and takes on the subject. But ultimately, your journey of exploring your hyper-local landscape of activism will be entirely unique. Lean into what feels good and nourishing.

Conventions and Conferences

There are places for exclusivity, such as at a conference where there is time set aside for queer or trans people to open up about deeply personal things, together. It goes without saying that support groups also fall into this category. Straight people should not make any attempt to come into places that are created specifically for queer and trans people to share with each other.

However, there are also events and spaces like the Philadelphia Trans Wellness Conference that are focused on LGBTQ people, but also have a shopping area. Here all people are welcome to patronize queer and trans-owned businesses and learn about supporting trans folks.

See if the LGBTQ events near you have a component like this. Then take that opportunity to support and get to know the queer-owned and queer-serving organizations in your community. They may want you there to support local business! Or nab you as a volunteer.

Drag Shows, Storytimes, Bars, and Meetups

As said earlier, there are some historic queer bars that might have a clientele that frowns on cis-het (cisgender, heterosexual) invasion. Again, it's about knowing your audience or, more simply, being respectful. Queers don't want your noisy, obnoxious bachelorette party, celebrating heterosexuality and alcoholism, taking over our queer space.

However, we are all, unfortunately, living under capitalism, so for the most part, a queer-owned bar or restaurant *does* want your support in the form of buying drinks and food—if you can offer it in a respectful way. Make sense?

I argue that cis folks should show up at LGBTQ venues

and events for all sorts of reasons. Their presence increases visibility for community events and services and drives traffic to them helping keep queer business owners and event promoters afloat. Another reason for allies to show up is to increase safety by being another body that can take a video or call for help if something shady goes down.

Allies can also be helpful in creating a safe, physical barrier for queer people to exist in. Your presence signals that these people (queers) are normal, and that being near them is normal and safe. This might be more of a rural concern, but I think that it can be helpful even in urban areas. Being a wing-person for your one queer friend in the bar is great. Doing the same thing for a queer bar takeover is even better. Your presence at a new drag show that is not yet well-established can help signal that hostile elements are not welcome. And it shows that you want these kinds of cultural events in your community!

It's so great that drag shows are infiltrating mainstream culture at this point. However, drag storytimes, which I love, are under attack. For years, local libraries across the county have partnered with local LGBTQ centers and performers to offer storytime for young ones presented by local drag performers. The benefits are numerous—gender non-conformity is normalized for young ones and families, and libraries increase engagement through novel and entertaining new ways to promote literacy. Unfortunately, the hypersexualization tactic of hate groups shows up often as a way to attack drag storytime. They use every tactic in the moral panic playbook to create fear and disgust by insinuating that drag performers are child predators by definition or that gender non-conformity spreads to unwilling participants like a contagion.

Funny thing is, I feel like combating the idea of hypersexualization is *exactly why* drag storytime came about: to counter the idea that existing in a different gender presentation is somehow perverse or predatory. It isn't. Defend drag storytime by explaining this.

Pride Parades, Celebrations, and Fairs

I'm especially touched when I hear stories or see pictures of queer people in rural areas who are experiencing a Pride event for the first time. I remember how freeing it felt to be safe *and* visible for the first time. To be seen. To be heard. To feel part of a tribe when in so much of life we can feel isolated.

How can you show up for your local Pride? There are a hundred and one ways. Can you:

- Donate money?

- Encourage your employer to fiscally sponsor the event?

- March, vend, or table at the event?

- Do face paint?

- Take pictures and videos and post them? Do a podcast episode there?

- Encourage the presence and importance of journalists?

- Share the event flyers on socials? Post the event flyer in your business?

- Show up to a city council meeting where Pride events or rainbow flag raising are being discussed and volunteer to speak up in support?

- Provide transportation to someone who needs it?

- Be a sober driver?

- Take videos of hateful counter protesters or harassers?

- Volunteer? (More on this in Chapter 9.)

These are some next-level ideas. Not everyone has the financial means, or the time, to donate to every effort. Use your time and resources wisely. And if you are doing queer justice work elsewhere, by all means, just celebrate at Pride! Just being there—increasing the numbers, increasing the witnesses—increases the fun and safety as a side effect.

Civic Actions

I think there is little argument that straight folks should show up for civic actions and protests on behalf of LGBTQ people. I'd go further and say that straight folks *need* to do the bulk of the work in this area. Increasingly, people are realizing that it should not be the burden of the minority, oppressed group to do all the fighting on its own behalf.

For example, in my small town for the last five years, the city council has staged an annual gladiatorial battle in which community members are forced to fight and argue for the necessity of raising the rainbow flag in June. They are put up against hateful community members who argue that LGBTQ people are in defiance of good, old Christian values and such. In my view, the stance with the largest number of voices wins. Help us by adding your voice.

Find opportunities for civic engagement on your city and county websites and social media. Nervous? Ask a friend to join you. Definitely go once just to observe and see how the meeting is run. Many city councils begin their meetings by giving any citizen three minutes to speak on any topic. Start imagining your three minute speech for next time.

PROTESTS

There are plenty of people taking action against hundreds of anti-trans bills right now and all the various injustices and murders and wars happening across the globe. There are probably more opportunities to show up and speak out on behalf of LGBTQ folks and other marginalized minorities than ever before. Instagram is the way that many young people are organizing. Facebook is also still used, but less so. If you want to stay in touch with what revolutionary young people are doing in your area, you probably need to get an Instagram account. You don't have to post anything or have much of a presence. But use it to follow queer, youth, or POC-led organizations in your area. This is where they post digital flyers about protests, teach-ins, and more.

There are tons of other books and 'zines about personal safety while protesting that I won't overlap with here; I also talk more about this in Chapter 10: Creating True Safe Spaces. But remember, in general take video of any harassment including police harassment (as long as you are not seen as interfering with their work), even if you have no idea how it might ever be used. You might be asked for it later by folks who will know what to do with it.

Remember: the right to peacefully protest is one of our most foundational rights in this country!

SCHOOL BOARD MEETINGS

Generally speaking, only parents and guardians with children attending the specific school district are expected to attend or speak up at school board meetings. However, my childless self has definitely been invited to speak at school board meetings to advocate for someone who had been harassed or denied dignity as a trans person.

If you have personal experience with kids who have been mistreated at school, experience serving queer and trans youth, or are friends of families who have, join them at school board meetings that have items that affect queer and trans kids on the agenda. This is best done with coordination with other groups of people who are speaking out in order to have a unified voice. My suggestion would be to reach out to your local LGBTQ organizations if you are interested in attending a school board meeting and try to meet up with others beforehand to strategize.

CITY COUNCIL MEETINGS

As mentioned before, city council meetings follow a specific formula. They usually begin with a public comment period where people can comment for three minutes on anything *not* on the agenda. But in our context, it's more likely that you will be showing up to a city council meeting with something *on the agenda*—like whether or not to raise a rainbow flag in the town square or to allow permits for Pride. In this case, find out where on the agenda your item is, usually marked by numbers or letters (e.g., agenda item 3B-25). Fill out a request to speak on that specific agenda item and wait until your name is called to speak.

Every city council will be different. Sometimes, they put the controversial item first to get it out of the way as quickly as possible. Other times, especially if they are hostile to the issue, they will put it last on the agenda, forcing the crowd to wait and sometimes speak until late in the evening, trying to starve you out. Bring water and snacks, just in case! Some cities allow people to call in a comment. They will then play the comment on the loudspeakers during the meeting. This is an effective way to participate, too.

In sum, show up! Show up to the rally. Show up to the art show. Show up to the performance. There is strength, safety, and fun in numbers. You may run into queer activists that will challenge your motives for being in queer spaces. Politely and clearly let them know the reasons for you being there. Are you there because you want to add your voice in support of queer initiatives? Because you want to increase safety at a protest? Because you want to start to be more directly involved in local justice? Articulating your "why" is an excellent exercise that builds your justice muscles going forward. So, never be afraid to take advantage of all the chances you can to protect, defend, educate, and enlighten folks about being an active ally. And don't forget that part of being an excellent ally is connecting with your local community of activists and learning what they feel are the most pressing issues and areas to work on in your part of the world.

CHAPTER 9

NEXT STEP UP: VOLUNTEERING

I t is *great* to show up to the march, the drag show, and the Pride parade, but now you want to take the next step. The next step up is volunteering.

Nonprofit organizations run on volunteer power. They are only as strong as those doing the work. Over the last seven years of being in this space, I've learned that the most important thing for a next-level ally to keep in mind when volunteering is to be consistent and dependable. Whatever it is that you choose to do, have great, two-way communication with those directing you. Speak honestly about your capacity and any changes in your availability. Not showing up to a planned event can have ripples of harm for the organization that has committed to being there.

Volunteers can help amplify our signal by just being at our community event tables. Or by helping others with rides to event opportunities. You might distribute posters and pamphlets letting people know who to call for help when they are in trouble. You might help us organize our contact list, help with social media and websites, and there is so much more.

Calling up your local LGBTQ nonprofit and asking if they need volunteers is a great idea! However, I want to share some of the other ways that you can deeply impact your local queer community. Your path will be unique. There are infinite possibilities for queer justice work. This chapter will explore some of the common possibilities you might be considering, and offer some you may not have thought of.

Local Social Justice Work

You might decide that the right option for you is to volunteer for social justice initiatives in your area that aren't necessarily queer-specific, but nonetheless intersect strongly with queer justice. Some examples include:

- A political campaign for a progressive candidate.

- A homeless shelter, especially one that is youth-focused.

- Advocates for foster youth (e.g., CASA).[17]

- Naloxone training and distribution.

- Suicide hotlines and local mental health response teams.

If you choose to volunteer for these kinds of initiatives, you are also secretly embedding yourself within the greater organization as a champion for queer justice. You can use this position to advocate for access to gender-neutral bathrooms, LGBTQ cultural sensitivity training, and stronger connections

---

17 If you volunteer in some capacity for homeless youth or foster youth, you can be sure you will be helping queer clients eventually. Queer people are disproportionately impacted by homelessness and overrepresented in foster care. You can also specifically request to be an advocate for a queer foster youth, although this is probably best left to LGBTQ-identifying people.

with local queer organizations. All while centering queer voices, of course. Here are a few other ways to make an impact locally.

Food Distribution

More and more often food distribution is done by a network of tiny community organizations and volunteers. Funding cuts to our local food bank forced them to rely on different community hubs for distribution years ago. Also, there is a growing movement to rescue food from landfills. This requires a roster of weekly volunteers to gather food from local businesses and grocery stores.

Performing food distribution activities aids all people, and you can bet queers are in that number, as well as immigrants, folks experiencing homelessness, and others who are increasingly under attack. If the result of you reading this book is you volunteering for a food bank or other food distribution or rescue service, that is queer justice. Check out what this looks like in your area.

Community Closet

Have clothes to donate? See if a local LGBTQ group already has a donation closet for people transitioning. Volunteer to organize said closet. Or, start a closet of your own, embedded . . . anywhere! Gather donations from around your community. You may or may not choose to designate your closet as being for LGBTQ people primarily. If you keep it open to the public, I think that's great. And you can be sure that queer people will frequent it, especially if you advertise it with local LGBTQ-centered orgs. Give extra, unwanted items to your local homeless shelter or domestic violence shelter.

LEGAL AID

Whether you are in a large or small community, you might have a legal aid organization that can be a potential ally for queers. If you are in a large urban area, you might have a national organization like Advocates for Trans Equality or the Transgender Law Center in your area. Or you might have a local chapter of the American Civil Liberties Union (ACLU) nearby. Is your local ACLU chapter involved in queer justice work already? Ask!

You also might have a hyper-local legal aid organization that is committed to providing some amount of pro bono work for marginalized groups like immigrants or tenants of color. Ask them if they are doing any queer justice work and how you can help. They may be providing help for people seeking to change their name and gender. The process of filing with your county court for name and gender changes can be surprisingly easy depending on your state. Maybe you can volunteer to help people through the process of filing for themselves.

The above suggestions are not necessarily embedded in queer spaces, but help to work towards queer justice. Focus your work on where you feel you will make the biggest impact. It doesn't necessarily have to have a rainbow painted directly onto it. Next, are some specifically LGBTQ-facing options that might be an option for you in your community.

Types of LGBTQ Nonprofits and Community-Based Organizations (CBO)

Look for local LGBTQ nonprofits and other CBOs in your area. If you are in an urban area, you will likely have choices. If you are in a rural area, you might find one that is nascent and struggling to be.

PRIDE AND EVENT ORGANIZERS

Many local queer justice groups are focused on creating and organizing Pride events and other social events for queers throughout the year. Some of these events are closed, such as support groups. Others are more open to the public like game or craft meetups. Some are youth focused.

Make an attempt to do some research on the different organizations in your area before committing. Not all LGBTQ organizations are created equally and you don't want to find yourself working for one that doesn't end up aligning with your values.

For example, if you have multiple queer orgs in your area, there was often an ideological split somewhere in their protohistory. People might attribute it to personality differences, but if you dig deep, oftentimes it was a more meaningful disagreement. I have seen groups split over the transphobia of older cis gays, support for Palestine or Israel, where to focus resources and time, and how employees or volunteers were treated. It can be hard to find the truth, but if you make a good faith effort, including gathering input from others in your community who have had direct experiences, that is the best you can do.

Also remember that it is OK for you to have an opinion and a moral stance. Not all queers have all the answers or speak for all people. Sometimes, it can end up being a tricky line to walk between following the lead of local queer orgs and having our own opinions on how to do the work. I'll continue to give you food for thought on this throughout the rest of this chapter.

Once you've found the organization you want to volunteer for, great! First, ask them about their needs. They may know immediately what they need you to do. Do what they need with humility, good spirit, and cheer. If you have better ideas on how to do things, great. But save that for a little bit later. Observe what queer leaders are focused on, and their "hows" and "whys." Get to know your community and their needs on a deeper level before trying to provide guidance, especially as a cis-het ally. If you find yourself disagreeing deeply with their methods or goals, maybe that means it's time to seek out a different org with different tactics and values.

Sometimes you will find a nascent organization that is not sure how to use an ally as a volunteer. Some things to suggest could be:

- If they are a youth-focused group, can you be a chaperone?

- Can you do clerical things like collect contact information at events and compile the data into a mailing list?

- Can you help make flyers for social media?

- Can you organize snacks or a potluck for meetings?

- Can you throw a fundraising bake sale?

No matter how you identify, don't storm in thinking you immediately know what is best. This only creates resistance. Observe and figure out how to use your energy strategically over time. A great litmus test for this is: Does the work feel fulfilling to you or draining, heartbreaking, and argumentative? Lean into the fulfilling work, as this is what is most sustainable.

LGBTQ Mental Health Advocates

Some LGBTQ nonprofits are built on grants that are made available from state or county mental health or public health agencies. These organizations can be focused on addressing substance use, preventing overdose through naloxone training, preventing HIV, providing support groups, or whatever is part of their grant agreement. Ask them how you might be able to volunteer. Can you volunteer to distribute free HIV/STI test kits? Teach people how to administer naloxone? Anyone can learn to administer naloxone—no medical certification required—and it is a great skill to learn and be able to teach others.

LGBTQ Health Clinics

LGBTQ-focused health clinics might not always have opportunities for volunteers. Many are part of a larger healthcare organization that can be obtuse. But others are smaller, grassroots organizations spearheaded by local queer social orgs. Does yours have opportunities to volunteer? Some cities have a recovery house for trans folks who have traveled to your area for surgery. Can you help them with shopping, transportation, or errands?

Leading Respectfully as an Ally

In 2019, I started the beginnings of an LGBTQ center in partnership with a local arts organization whose property was owned and subsidized by the city. For three years, in preparation for the grand opening, I ran support groups, trained support facilitators, organized a board, built a roster of volunteers to staff the front desk, created promotional materials, and applied for grants from the city and county. By the time the org was off the ground, I was already feeling burnt out by the years of solid organizing without pay. I was working as a freelancer at the time, and it just so happened that my last contract didn't get paid for five months. So, I ended up taking a travel nursing contract out of state to make quick money, and get a break from advocacy.

Immediately after I left for my nursing gig, a straight, cis ally whom we had brought on as a volunteer—we explicitly did *not* make her a board member because we valued our 100% queer board as it was—used political maneuvering and amplified certain personality conflicts to split the board, and suggest that she should take over as CEO! Her argument was that the organization should be run more like a business and that she was the most savvy businessperson involved in the organization. Though she claimed to be a unifier, she ousted queer leaders and led the org for the next three years.

During this time, she also managed to co-opt the organizing of Pride from a different, local LGBTQ org. Three years later, the programs I put in place at the art center are essentially unchanged, though they are now unfunded and not sustainable for the future. And our Pride, which in 2019 was an out-and-loud parade up and down Main Street, is now relegated to a small park and not well attended. And to top it all off, she herself has left town.

It goes without saying, don't be that kind of ally. But I tell the story to illustrate the rationale. People who aren't LGBTQ are not, by definition, in touch intuitively with what queer people want and need in their hyper-local communities. Therefore, they are not going to be able to create innovative solutions for queers. They might attempt to overlay strategies and systems that work for straight people onto the ways queer people want to organize and lead. These strategies might not resonate with people who are exploited and marginalized by said systems. Oftentimes, we have to dream up whole new systems for ourselves.

Also illustrated here is a misguided effort to consolidate all LGBTQ services in the county into one organization. While there is strength in numbers in many ways, this is not actually a strategic goal in and of itself. Why? Gathering multiple partners into a coalition is usually the more strategic move. An org with lots of community partners is more attractive to grants and governments. This also makes room for different strategies and dissenting opinions.

If you find yourself silencing dissent, you are not being a good ally. If you are consolidating power for its own sake, you are not being an ally. If you are talking louder than the local queers, you are not being an ally. You also aren't acting strategically or usefully. Queers are simply going to be more invested long-term in the work and solutions than straight allies who will eventually get tired of the drama and effort. It's not their life they are fighting for, after all. Following the lead of local queers ends up being the only sustainable solution.

Spearheading Queer Initiatives

Allies can still be strategic and innovative, especially in rural areas with nascent movements. Allies can leverage the resources available to them to help organize space for queer events. Know a cafe or bar owner? Have a conversation with them about holding LGBTQ events in partnership with a local org. If they are resistant, ask why? Have a respectful conversation, even if it happens over weeks or years.

Are you in HR? You can start an LGBTQ affinity resource group and see who shows up. See if you can identify queer-identified leadership just by advertising the opportunity. Make sure there are policies whereby managers are obligated to give their staff time to attend.

Are you an educator? See Chapter 11 on starting a GSA in the absence of queer leadership at your school. Start a meetup, and then let queer students take the lead.

Change happens slowly; start now, and from all angles. Just putting the idea in someone's head for them to consider is a very important first step. Don't force the issue. Just patiently open the dialogue.

JOINING THE BOARD

Do you have specialized skills? Queer orgs need you for their board! Show up to some board meetings and humbly but confidently state the skills you have and ask how you can be useful. Some examples of in demand skills are:

- Bookkeeping or accounting. Please help us as treasurer or help create an annual report!

- Organizational. Please be our board secretary! Or organize our contact list for mailings or text alerts.

- Grant writer. It goes without saying that you can help local queer orgs become more sustainable with your grant writing skills.

- Website building skills.

- Social media skills. Trust me, everyone needs help here, as the work is endless.

Queer organizers need you.

If they have limits on the number of people on their boards or teams who don't identify as LGBTQ, that is OK, accept it with grace. Ask if you can provide these services as a regular member or volunteer. Don't get power hungry even if you think you have really good ideas.

Follow the Lead of Local Queers

In short, identify queer leaders within your spheres of influence and ask yourself how you can support them. Can you give them a space, a voice, or a platform? Can you bring queer programming and presenters into your theater, gallery, library, classroom? Can your nonprofit be a fiscal sponsor for a new queer org?

To hammer the point home, be forceful, be a leader, but alongside your local queer organizers. Bring your unique energy, but ask folks what they need and how they envision you showing up for that. Make space for queers, then let them direct things.

Volunteer happily and with a smile, putting a positive face to the organization. Even *that* does so much. Bring your mom or grandma with you as you volunteer or table at Pride. Bring the happy and the wholesome (if that is your thing). As people's first impressions and off-hand opinions flood the internet, they have surprising ripple effects. Give people positive first impressions. Put a rainbow ripple in the pond.

Let's get this done.

Radical Inclusivity

For straights *and* queers starting organizations, I encourage you to do some thinking about radical inclusivity. I find doing deep thinking about inclusivity and how to give voice to folks who often don't have one can often be overlooked—especially by queers or organizers who suddenly find themselves with a platform, an elected position, a grant, a space, or some other kind of new voice and power in their community. Living in the capitalist hellscape as we all are, it is now natural to turn defensive and inadvertently harm others who we fear might compromise our newfound voice and position.

I feel it is absolutely crucial to mindfully operate from a solid bedrock of inclusivity for everyone you touch in your community, as liberation cannot come for only a few. A well-known example that has been written about elsewhere by many smart people is the phenomenon of trans people being excluded from organizing spaces that feel our non-conformity might harm their efforts to appear respectable and professional. You should Google "trans-exclusionary radical feminists" (TERFs) and the story of Sylvia Rivera and her Street Transvestite Action Revolutionaries if you do not immediately know what I am talking about.

However, TERFs are not the only consideration. For example, how does your organization include the voice and participation of people experiencing homelessness in your area? How do you treat people who smell bad who come into your center? How about people who may have poor boundaries and communication skills due to mental health challenges, who spam your inbox, or share the same comments week after week during your meetings? Do you exclude or find ways to include? What if you find out a volunteer has been "borrowing" supplies from your center, like toilet paper or snacks they couldn't afford that week?

These are important value discussions to have within your organizations and communities, not purely from an inclusivity angle, but also for sustainability. I've seen organizations and centers implode because volunteers and community members disagreed on how to approach these topics.

Personally, I think it makes sense, and it's also strategic, to operate from the position that no one can achieve liberation unless everyone is liberated. Therefore, struggles of all marginalized people are linked, and we all must work together with a shared purpose in every possible way. In the next sections, I will share some concepts and ideas around inclusivity for you to sit with and consider in your work.

ELEVATING AND INCLUDING PARTNER ORGANIZATIONS

Aligning with other local organizations—not only those exclusively serving LGBTQ people—is strategic. So create a web of care that includes food banks, homeless shelters, organizations devoted to mental health advocacy, immigrant rights, legal aid, youth, and more. Creating and advertising this web helps the local queer community understand which groups are welcoming to queers and which might not be.

For example, not all queers might feel comfortable approaching faith-based organizations for food or healthcare. Sometimes this is for good reason. Some churches use charity outreach as an opportunity to proselytize. Some front-line staff are just plain disgusted by queer-looking people. Some of us may have had bad experiences with religious groups in our past.

But if you know that a certain faith-based organization *is* actually welcoming to all people, let folks know. Publicize their food distribution events on your LGBTQ org's social media. Partner with legal aid orgs who offer services to low-income queers. A network of organizations with shared goals is the most sustainable way to build community.

Compassion and Mental Illness

Queer people are disproportionately affected by mental health challenges, including eating disorders, substance use disorders, and suicidal thinking and attempts.[18] Radically inclusive orgs should partner with other nonprofits or their county mental health organizations to have your volunteers and staff trained in mental health de-escalation principles and techniques. All the better if they have a mobile response unit that can help out in tense situations, instead of calling the police. Your local landscape of mental healthcare will be unique.

People suffering from moderate to severe mental illness might act compulsively, disturb group dynamics, spam your messages, and hyperfocus on real or imagined threats and persecution. How does your organization fare in terms of education and compassion on these topics? Can you create an environment with strong boundaries that allow people with mental illness to participate? Or will they be excluded?

Sometimes, your local county mental health and public health agencies can bring a variety of educational seminars to not only your staff, but your group participants. For example, in my role as facilitator for my transgender support group, I partnered with the local public health department to come give talks on stress and depression. Everyone loved it—and it built trust across both groups. Get to know what your local organizations can offer you.

Another great place to look for tools to create safe spaces for everyone is NAMI—the National Alliance on Mental Illness. You may have a chapter near you that is happy to provide education on these subjects, including training people on how

---

18 Chan, "Investigating the Interrelationships."

to run a safe and inclusive support group. Inviting NAMI to come speak to your group about how to support someone experiencing psychosis could be a memorable and educational connection for all.

Unnecessary Police Interactions Can Re-Traumatize

An important concept to keep in mind is avoiding calling the cops on people experiencing a mental health crisis unless there is real threat of bodily harm about to happen. Oftentimes, folks experiencing some kind of psychosis will talk or yell loudly or gesticulate wildly, making some folks nervous. But more often than not, psychotic behavior does not lead to random acts of violence. More often, people are waving away things they are seeing in their mind that we can't see or yelling at people who are not there. These people are not a threat to your group or event, and generally have no reason to be of police attention. If you have a mental health response team in your community, call them. If not, find a way to direct the person to a place of safety, and away from your group, if you can. Ask for help. Mental illness is sadly familiar to so many of us, and a participant from your group or event might offer crucial redirection help.

Think about these things before they happen, and reach out to others to formulate a plan.

Keep in mind that queer folks may have had interactions with police or mental health institutions in the past that were traumatic and unaffirming. I have a friend who is a trans woman who was held in a locked psychiatric facility for a time. She stated that the staff refused to help or allow her to shave which resulted in humiliating beard growth. This was around 2020. Unfortunately, there is no shortage of stories of this kind of treatment. A paper published in the *International Journal of*

Nursing Studies in 2025[19] details stories about gender-affirming practices being withheld in mental institutions and a recent article on the Marshall Project website[20] describes trans women being forced to show their breasts to prison staff so they can determine whether or not they will be allowed to wear a bra.

Please be compassionate towards folks who may have been traumatized by police and policing institutions in the past. Next-level allies think about this before they act.

People Experiencing Homelessness

Queer people, especially youth, are disproportionately affected by homelessness. Multiple studies continue to show that up to 40% of young people experiencing homelessness are LGBTQ.[21] Anything you can do to ally yourself with your local homeless services and outreach, especially for youth, is queer justice.

With that in mind, people experiencing homelessness may want to take part in queer events. All people, queer or straight, might hold negative stereotypes about people experiencing homelessness. Conflict can arise when people are not bathed well, wear unwashed clothes, or take large portions or hoard food. Meet any conflict with compassion. Remind people that you are here to serve all people, and some people have greater needs than others. Do everything you can to create a safe space for those experiencing homelessness. Life is hard enough as it is.

19 Kristen D. Clark et al., "'I Don't Think I Have Been Out of Fight or Flight. Ever.' Transgender People's Experiences in Inpatient Psychiatric Treatment," *International Journal of Nursing Studies,* 165 (May 2025), https://doi.org/10.1016/j.ijnurstu.2025.105028.

20 Beth Schwartzapfel, "New Florida Policy on Trans Care in Prison like 'Conversion Therapy,'" The Marshall Project, December 10, 2024, https://www.themarshallproject.org/2024/12/10/new-florida-prison-policy-on-trans-health-care-like-conversion-therapy.

21 Trevor Goodyear et al., "Intersecting Transitions Among 2S/LGBTQ+ Youth Experiencing Homelessness: A Scoping Review," *Children and Youth Services Review,* (2024), https://doi.org/10.1016/j.childyouth.2023.107355.

Being a great volunteer and ally may not seem simple. But ultimately, it really is. Above all, act with humility and optimism at all times. Defer to the queer leaders and the community you are serving, since they are the ones that know best about what they need. Lean into compassion for those you might encounter who have had a tough life. Ask for and accept constructive criticism. Lean into what feels good, easy, and not contentious. If you find yourself having a lot of disagreements and trying to make a lot of structural changes, find another agency that more aligns with the kind of work you are best at. Go with the flow!

CHAPTER 10

CREATING TRUE SAFE SPACES

*I*f you have, or are considering, signage at your workplace or organization proclaiming it to be a "safe space," what does that mean to you? What does that mean for people when they cross your threshold? What can they expect? How will they be addressed? Treated? Served? Can you guarantee that?

A safe space is a place that can safely and lovingly hold queers experiencing mental illness, poor coping, and housing and food insecurity. A place where queers and their public displays of affection are whole-heartedly supported. Where their gender non-conforming ways of dressing and doing makeup, hair, and nails are the norm. What if I, a man with a small goatee, piercings, and short hair, came into your shop wearing a skirt? Would your staff compliment me or try their best to ignore me?

The phrase "safe space" can connote a space where people feel emotionally safe to do and say what is in their hearts. But it is also a physical space that is safe for all people to be in. In the previous chapters, I mention when allies show up to events it can help make the event safer by increasing the number of people (witnesses) and creating physical barriers around people. This is because when talking about creating safe spaces we unfortunately also have to talk about violence in our society. Trans and non-binary people face the threat of violence everyday; we face a higher risk of murder, harassment, and bullying than the average person.[22] As a result, trans and non-binary people often have a heightened awareness of the threat of violence or harassment. Regardless of how safe you perceive your community to be, violence is always a possibility.

This chapter will dive into what it means to create spaces that are truly safe as can be for all—emotionally and physically. I will talk about different kinds of spaces you might be holding for queers and the different considerations that come up for each. Sadly, in this era, that means talking about open spaces, closed spaces, and the threat of an active shooter event. But first, a few notes on creating spaces where people feel safe to share openly.

Ground Rules

For any event, whether it is open to allies or just for queers, it's important to have a set of ground rules and guiding principles. This works for classrooms, book clubs, discussion groups of all kinds, gaming events, and so on. For me, it is a must-have for the support groups and events for youth I run.

Ground rules can be as simple as signage that clearly states, "All are welcome here." This message sets the tone and general expectations. It makes hate unwelcome, and a certain amount of hateful people will self-edit out of spaces that set this expectation in writing. But ground rules can also take the form of *a set of*

22 Andrew R. Flores et al., "Gender Identity Disparities in Criminal Victimization: National Crime Victimization Survey, 2017-2018," *American Journal of Public Health,* (April 2021), https://ajph.aphapublications.org/doi/10.2105/AJPH.2020.306099.

rules that everyone agrees to when they participate in your event. You can make this explicit via a sign in sheet, meaning when a participant signs in they are agreeing to your group rules, or you can read out the rules before the event begins.

Here are my rules for groups and events that I have used, and refined, over many years.

PEER SUPPORT GROUP AGREEMENT

By signing in to this peer-led support group, you agree to the following:

1. **Confidentiality.** At no time in conversation or on social media will I discuss any of the particular members of the group in any identifiable way: I will not speak about their looks, manner of dress, names or occupations, their partners, or things they said. What's said here, stays here.

2. Partners or parents may be invited to attend with unanimous agreement from the group. **This group is NOT an educational event for partners, i.e. partners will not ask questions of the group.** Partners may learn quietly and passively by listening. Partners and parents are absolutely bound by all of the other relevant rules listed here. Partners and parents may be asked to leave at any time at the discretion of the facilitator. This is to ensure that no group member feels the responsibility to educate.

3. **Listen fully.**

4. Speak using first person "I" language.

5. Only talk about group members that are present, with respect.

6. Hostility will be defined as speaking about committing violence, transphobic, homophobic or racist comments, talking over someone already speaking, refusing to respect pronouns, and/or repeatedly denying or dismissing the experience of another. We are here to learn about a variety of experiences and everyone's unique experience is valid. **Persons engaging in any hostile or dismissive behavior may be asked to leave, either for that session or permanently, as per the discretion of the facilitator.** This is to ensure that all participants feel safe and encouraged to share honestly.

Feel free to use any or all of this example when crafting ground rules and expectations for your safe space. Support group rules are a bit extra by definition. Feel free to craft yours more gently.

Once you have expectations set, it is so much easier to step in when we see bullying, offensive, or other behaviors that are making people uncomfortable. Just point to the group agreement and remind people that they need to interact respectfully in order to continue participating in the group. Simple.

Creating Safe Closed Spaces

Libraries, LGBTQ centers, identity-based support groups, and classrooms are examples of small spaces that, even if closed to anyone except participants, can also be accessed by the public and potentially hostile people. How can we best keep our communities safe? The first thing to do is start a safety conversation at your organization.

Start talking about a plan and what you would really do

if someone came in with a weapon. Even just the exercise of visualizing that is *hugely* helpful. Get in a group and ask your staff and leadership, together, what they would do if someone came in with a gun. If you get entirely different answers from everyone, or sheer confusion, that tells you it is time to make a plan everyone is on board with. During an emergency, everyone needs to have the same idea about what to do.

Don't let the scary nature of the topic delay or stall your plans to talk with your group. Every building that is open to the public should have all kinds of emergency plans including an active shooter plan. Consultants who have training from the Department of Homeland Security (DHS) can help your organization create one. Your local Red Cross might be a good place to start searching for this kind of training.

The following table outlines safety training resources you may want to consider for your organization. If this is scary for you to think about, good! All the more reason to research each one and demystify what it can potentially accomplish for you. Anyone can be trained to create an emergency plan for a building.

SAFETY TRAINING TABLE

TYPE OF TRAINING OR MODULE	PURPOSE AND DESCRIPTION	WHO USES IT
Active Shooter Plan or Training (ASAPP, ALICE, AVIRT)	Train staff and volunteers to stay as safe as possible during a mass shooting event	Large organizations with large buildings—but anyone can make a plan and get trained

Stop the Bleed	Save lives after a shooting, accident, or disaster	First responders and disaster responders
Emergency Medicine	Apply effective first aid	Anyone!
Self-Defense	Learn to defend yourself effectively from physical attacks and disarm attackers	Anyone!
Managing Assaultive Behavior (MAB)	Learn to quickly repel and escape from violence	Healthcare professionals and Mental health professionals
Professional Assault Crisis Training (Pro-ACT)	Learn to quickly contain and escape from violence	Teachers and recovery home staff
Crisis Prevention Institute (CPI)	Hands-off crisis de-escalation techniques	Teachers and recovery home staff
Applied Suicide Intervention Skills Training (ASIST)	Learn how to effectively open a conversation about suicide and best practices for keeping people safe	Mental health professionals
Mental Health First Aid	Learn how to compassionately respond to people experiencing crisis	Disaster responders, Red Cross volunteers, NAMI volunteers

Your local county mental health organization may offer ASIST or MAB training periodically, and they may be free to the public. Your local chapter of NAMI might offer training regarding how to compassionately respond to people experiencing mental health crises. A local Red Cross office is a good place to ask about any of these kinds of training; they may be able to point you to a consultant who can help you create an active shooter plan, for example. Doesn't hurt to ask!

Also, there are more and more locally owned MMA and other kinds of combat gyms around the country. Sometimes they offer self-defense courses open to the public. Some LGBTQ organizations have partnered with these organizations to offer self-defense training sessions specifically for queer people. Is this a partnership that might work for your agency and community? Do you have the space and ability to host a self-defence class for queers at your agency? That would be a very next-level thing to bring to your community.

Safety at Large Public Events

Deadly public violence is unpredictable. But this doesn't mean that there aren't things we can do to proactively make our community gatherings safer.

In the next section, I'll summarize some of the things I've learned through many days and hours of training with the Red Cross and DHS. Disclaimer: this is not a substitute for getting trained yourself! The idea behind this chapter is to demystify the issue and get real conversations started about keeping everyone safe in a crowded public situation. Organisers can often find it very difficult to bring up this topic with their fellow event planners. It's scary! However, it is even more scary to be confronted with an emergency that threatens your participants and volunteers with no plan in place. Whether you are planning a zinefest at the local library, an ICE protest at your nearby highway overpass, or a full downtown Pride parade you should start a safety conversation with your fellow organizers and the facility managers, if applicable.

De-Escalation and Protests

You may have community orgs in your area who are already trained and experienced in de-escalation tactics during protests (Pride is thought of as a protest event by many). It might be smart to ally yourself and make connections with local, radical orgs like the Brown Berets. They may be able to provide specific training on de-escalation and otherwise avoiding and subverting hate and violence while out in the streets. Locally, I recently partnered with them to host a protest safety training which included de-escalation, personal safety, and basic first-aid training. It is outside of the scope of this book to talk in depth about protest safety, but there are more resources now online than ever before. Some good sources on this can be found on Greenpeace, MoveOn, and Indivisible websites. As I've said before, there might be other orgs in your area interested in this topic, so team up with them for training and keep the whole community safer.

Confronting Uncomfortable Situations and Interrupting Public Hate

Say you are at a Pride event. You know that it is generally a place of revelry, color, happiness, and celebration, if not downright debauchery. Say you see someone dressed drably, visibly uncomfortable, perhaps sneering or hostile appearing. Say you are worried they have a weapon. In short, you find them suspicious. But you do not see them wielding any actual weapon or threatening anybody. What do you do?

You might think about looking around for a police officer or someone with authority. But while this might be a good move in some cases, in a lot of cases it is not. For one, the person could disappear into the crowd before you ever find the authority figure you are looking for. Another reason is that police and security officers are trained to respond in specific ways to specific situations, and this can lead to unnecessary violence or avoidable escalation of a situation, simply by how people culturally respond to cops. And, statistically speaking, it is highly unlikely that you will identify someone with dangerous intent *and* a concealed weapon at a random large, public event like a Pride parade. So, we want to avoid causing any unnecessary panic or targeting someone who is simply uncomfortable!

In most situations, the better thing to do is to actually approach the person with the forceful customer service attitude we learned about in previous chapters. So useful!

A person intending on doing harm, or researching a place he intends to do harm, is nervous. Even if they are completely convinced that what they are planning on doing is just, they still fear either failing at their objective one way or another or being caught and punished. So, approaching someone acting nervous and suspicious with a big, loud, "Hi! Are you lost? How can I help you?" can be completely unnerving to them. It lets them know you see them. It lets them know that people are watching and that maybe this isn't the easy target they were hoping for.

I've used this tactic to dissuade people who have come to a Pride event to counter-protest or simply show their general displeasure with whatever is going on. This does not just have to be used only to deter a possible threat of violence. It can be very meaningful to publicly and loudly other and alienate those who are there to bully or shame your group. I enjoy confronting people with a "Hey! Enjoying the show?" Or, "Hello! What brings you here today? I'm here to support trans rights. Isn't this GREAT?"

Letting hateful people know that they are in the minority, and making them uncomfortable about it, is an incredibly just and powerful thing to do. They might give you a sneer. But usually, it's as they are leaving. People who hate are generally cowards who pick on lone individuals. They will not stand up to a united group of people who loudly protect one another and watch out for each other.

You can seldom go wrong asking "Hey, how are you? Can I help out?" It will unnerve those in the wrong and uplift those that are in the right.

The same goes for interrupting harassment and bullying that you witness in public. Come at them with that forceful customer-service attitude like: "Hi! Everything alright here?" Nothing wrong with asking, right? Try to do it with a big smile to signal that you are just there to help and not assuming anything is going on. Try to look the victim in the eye and ask, "Are you OK?" If you're told to get lost, great! Just give a smile and a "Just making sure!"

Remember, asking if everything is alright is *never* the wrong move.

But if someone does *not* respond that everything is alright, if they look away or withdraw, that could be your cue to step in more and ask that person directly if they feel comfortable. If they can't answer, let the bully know in clear terms that "It looks like you are making this person uncomfortable."

What happens next depends on the situation, your comfort in confrontation, and your personal ability. Are you a big and confident person who is able to put physical space between the bully and the victim? Are you able to ask others for help? Can you point out what is happening to the bus driver or some kind of nearby authority? Are you comfortable getting out your phone and recording?

What you will do from here will be personalized, and no one tactic fits all. But one or more of the above strategies is usually enough to get a bully embarrassed enough with the attention to walk away. Bullies know what they are doing is considered wrong by most people. The problem is that they also know that most people don't speak up. So, a lone faggot is a great target.

KAYLEE'S STORY

Kaylee (pseudonym) was a trans woman on the small side. I met her when she was the subject of a portrait in a group exhibit I had put together. She came to the exhibition opening and we had a chat in the galleries. She was living in Stockton, California, and had recently been assaulted on a bus. She was eager to share her story, and gave me permission to share it along with pictures of her black and blue face on our LGBTQ org's social media.

Kaylee had been loudly taunted on the public bus in front of many witnesses. When she got off, she was followed and beaten up. When I reached out to ask if she wanted to share more details about her story for this book, I learned that she died of a fentanyl overdose a few years back.

This is the piece she wrote for the art show that featured her portrait:

Why should people have to judge people when they are not sure about themselves?

Myself, I think gender and pronouns are the most important things you can approach someone with, like instead of saying 'sir' or 'ma'am,' just say "hello, how is your day?" instead of assuming what someone's pronouns or gender are.

I was born in Lodi and raised in a Republican city. About five years ago I moved to Stockton and a year ago I began hormones. I've known I was trans since I was around three years old. Since my move, I've been advocating for transgender rights and for my community. I'm happy now. If people say, "Oh you're a tranny," I just sit and smile. What other people say or do doesn't matter.

I believe that everyone should know their rights, especially people who are disabled or have special needs. Sometimes disabled people don't know their rights, and I think it's important to support all members of our community. I'm beginning to start my own group for transgender and LGBT people with disabilities.

Be bold enough to use your voice, brave enough to listen to your heart, and strong enough to live the life you've always imagined.

When I spoke with her family about adding her story to this book, her aunt had this to add:

As a lil' one she just wanted to be accepted. Bullied a lot in grade school so much she threatened to blow up the school in an outburst . . . At her high school graduation, I was afraid no one would cheer when her name was called, but she got a standing ovation! I tear up now thinking about it. She had her protectors and also her bullies.

Then at a party after graduation she was roofied and assaulted . . . . [She] was arrested in mid 20s for drug possession . . . moved in with a family friend who she confided in about what she wanted to be happy. She was encouraged by friends to go through with the transition and she was all in. She had all the support and said she was happy . . .

But sadly that support fell away from her . . . . All those that encouraged her were gone and she was left to defend herself. The drugs became worse. Couch-hopping, not taking meds, growing a beard back . . . . Her boyfriend and I went to the local LGBTQ club in Stockton and tried to get her into a rehab but she refused to go . . . . At the end she was actually bragging about using fentanyl and that's what got her. All her years of physical, mental, emotional torment died on the bathroom floor of a laundry mat.

We will never know for sure if Kaylee would have been saved from beaten black and blue if a bystander on the bus had spoken up, but to me, it does sound like a very reasonable assumption. Once it is announced that there is someone being victimized, people mobilize to help. I've seen it enough after hundreds of hours riding subway cars and walking the streets of Manhattan and Brooklyn while travel-nursing for two years. People are interested in justice. They just have to understand what is happening. Once someone calls out bullying, others step in to the victim's defense. Literally no one likes a bully.

Just being the one to call it "bullying," to call out what is happening—I can't stress how powerful that is. After it's called out, others circle around, and pile on in their own ways to make a bully uncomfortable. Once they know they are outnumbered and being watched, they generally stop.

Let them know that people are watching, and we don't approve.

CHAPTER 11

NEXT-LEVEL EDUCATORS, SCHOOL ADMINISTRATORS, AND PARENTS

The next few chapters will focus on a few different career areas and offer specific ways that you can start moving the needle towards justice in your neck of the woods. This chapter is specifically about supporting young people in a school setting, and it's for next-level education professionals of all kinds (teachers, aides, administrators, librarians, tutors) and parents. You have very special roles to play, indeed! Keeping the most vulnerable of us safe is a full-time job, and it can feel like the expectations are changing faster than we can track. Trusting your gut and knowing the law are the two main points you need to practice to keep kids safe and support them at school.

Let Trans Kids Play Sports

Things are moving so quickly regarding trans inclusion in sports that anything specific I write today in early 2026 could easily become outdated in weeks or months. So I will speak broadly and briefly. Stand up for trans kids, and really, all trans people, when you can, where you can, on our inclusion in sports. Most recent attacks on us playing sports focus on banning trans women and girls in particular—another example of the pervasiveness of male privilege, and the pure ugliness and discrimination baked into their attack strategy.

There is no reason to exclude young people who are taking hormone blockers or gender-affirming hormone therapy from playing sports alongside any gender. Gender-affirming therapy for trans women and girls features testosterone suppression with a goal of getting it near zero. There is no evidence that trans girls taking gender-affirming therapy have any sports advantage over cis girls.

Often, once you start testosterone suppression you feel weaker within a matter of weeks. Recently, I shared an old story about a trans woman friend of mine to a young trans woman I just met. She instantly recognized and affirmed she had the same experience. Basically, my friend had to move into a new apartment soon after she had begun hormone therapy. She packed up her belongings one week and two weeks later she could no longer move the boxes she herself had originally packed.

It is heartbreaking to deny teens gender-affirming therapy, making them go through the puberty they never wanted in the first place, *and also* ban them from sports outright. Imagine being a trans teenager who is both not allowed to take puberty blockers (medications that have been prescribed safely to cis girls for decades for precocious puberty) and not allowed to play the sport they love because they're swimming in the testosterone they never wanted in the first place. In a better world, they would be allowed to go through female puberty and play alongside girls—there would be no reason not to.

On top of this, lawmakers and hateful activists complain about the paucity of research on gender-affirming care and sports while simultaneously defunding trans research.

Not being allowed to play sports limits trans' kids participation in society. As a next-level ally, please do what you can, where you can, to defend and protect trans women and girls. (As I referred to earlier, you can look up Mack Beggs's story for another example of this.)

Interrupting Bullies at School

The Trevor Project's 2024 U.S. National Survey on the Mental Health of LGBTQ+ Young People[23] found that *half* of queer young people participating reported bullying in the past year, a *third* of them seriously considered suicide, and more than 1 in 10 had attempted suicide.

In the United States, *everyone has the right to feel safe at school,* and this includes being safe from all harassment, verbal to physical. Historically, this was seen as guaranteed by Title IX, which is a federal law prohibiting discrimination based on sex in schools. I say historically because the federal government in 2025 is actively arguing on several different fronts that Title IX should not protect the rights of transgender youth. The result is that so much LGBTQ bullying doesn't get reported. Why? Sometimes, people aren't sure if something qualifies as bullying in the school policies. Your job as a next-level ally is to be crystal clear on your school's policies on the subject and how you are expected to enforce them.

23 "2024 U.S. National Survey on the Mental Health of LGBTQ+ Young People," The Trevor Project, accessed February 22, 2026, https://www. thetrevorproject.org/survey-2024/.

Queer, Gay, and "No Homo"

Kids will always find new and inventive ways to circumvent rules and expectations. But kids and adults alike can all instinctively understand when someone is using a word in a hurtful way. Kids using "gay" or "queer" in a derogatory way need to be called out. This can and should include being called out in front of their class. A discussion needs to be had about respectful language at school. This also applies to "no homo," another thinly veiled slur.

This doesn't only apply to a kid calling another kid "gay" in a hateful way. This also applies to using "gay" in the place of "stupid" or "boring." Letting this kind of language slide in the classroom and on the playground perpetuates a culture where queer people do not feel comfortable being themselves and participating at school.

Some kids will adopt gay, queer, lesbian, or trans as a self-identifier early on. This is great. Kids that can use these words and speak openly about their own experience are on the right track. Their friends and peers might use the same words around them with affection. That's great and should not be interrupted.

But confident kids can also be thrown off track by bullying just like everyone else. Just because they project strength and confidence one year, doesn't mean that will last into the next. One of the more heartbreaking scenarios I have watched play out is kids exploring their gender identity with fearlessness when young, adopting a queer or non-binary identity, but then deciding in the following years that "it's just too hard" (direct quote from someone under 10).

What kind of rules and values guide your classroom interactions? What are your classroom policies regarding respectful speech? Are they posted? How often do you talk about them? Is there specific language protecting queer kids in there? Why not?

OUTRIGHT SLURS AND BULLYING

Be clear that calling someone a faggot, calling someone an "it," or misgendering or misnaming people is stepping on their right to a safe education; it must be addressed in the same way that using any other hate-based slur would be addressed. If the bullies using the word faggot are not addressed in the same way that a child or teen using race-based hate speech would be, the school is in violation of the child's civil rights. It's as plain as that.

I've seen this escalate. People are very interested in justice. And when students see justice being applied unevenly this can lead to escalated student protest and unrest, often outweighing the instigating event. I've seen students mobilize and rightly blame school administration for condoning hate by punishing the victim (who was sent home after being shoved to the ground in the hall, for example) rather than the perpetrators.

How do you interrupt bullying you see on campus? Do you report it? Do the perpetrators see punishment?

Is the victim made to feel like this won't happen again? *Can* you assure the victim this won't happen again? If not, why not? And what can you do about it? Think about this, especially if you are a school administrator. Does your bullying policy explicitly prohibit anti-LGBTQ sentiments? If not, can you add a clause? Adding that clause, and sending out an announcement of the change, is possibly the strongest way to send a message about culture change at your institution. What other ways do you explicitly address bullying at your school?

But overall, remember, if you see a potentially hostile

situation, don't be afraid to approach it and ask in an aggressively friendly way, "Everything OK here?" This signals that you are a watchful ally, and you never know what response you might get and what impact you might make in someone's day (or year). This goes for all staff at any school.

Encourage Students to Report Bullying

Sometimes bullying isn't reported because there is a belief that the administration doesn't care about LGBTQ bullying and won't enforce rules equally or punish the perpetrators. Sometimes, that belief is well-founded. The administration may indeed be apathetic or hostile towards queer student complaints. The thing is, this is actually *even more* reason to report bullying at school.

A defense I've heard school administrators use when confronted with accusations of being protective of bullies is, "We've never gotten any complaints about that, before." So, an official complaint needs to be made. A track record needs to be documented. No one will ever get any footing without the first person who speaks up.

Filing a Report

If a student, or your child, comes to you with a report about being called a slur in the hallway, what next? The following section is for students, parents, and teachers who may be unfamiliar with filing a report; it outlines common procedures for escalating a complaint. Your school site might have unique rules, policies, and procedures—so definitely research what those are and follow them.

File a Complaint with the Title IX Coordinator

If your school has a Title IX coordinator, they are usually your first stop when making a report. It is their responsibility to investigate claims of bullying and harassment. They are meant to gather information and are forbidden from making determinations or passing judgment. Tell them everything that happened, with as much factual detail as possible. Tell them exactly what was said, when, and where. If someone pushed you, say that. If a teacher overheard or witnessed, tell them that.

File a Complaint with the School's Administration

If the results of this are not satisfactory, encourage kids and parents to file a general complaint. Every student, parent, or organization has the right to file a complaint and the right to receive a written resolution.

Counsel kids and parents to be brief, clear, and concise when writing their complaint. The complaint should clearly state what is being asked for and what justice would look like. Advise parents, if they are involved, to hold folks accountable. This is the hard part. Follow up every week until they get a response. If the result is unsatisfactory, the next step can be to bring it up at a school board meeting.

File a Complaint with the State Department of Education

If the resolution from the school administration is not satisfactory, then the victim can file a complaint with their State Department of Education. Sometimes this is the only way to get a school to start to change its culture. Nothing will change if unpunished bullying continues to go unaddressed.

File an Office of Civil Rights Complaint

If a student doesn't receive restorative or meaningful action from their State Board of Education regarding civil rights, they can file a complaint with the Department of Health and Human Services Office of Civil Rights. States often have a local branch.

The complaint generally has to come from the student themself. This can feel like a daunting task to a teenager. It is not right that our systems and society put the onus on the victims to do all the work. But this is the system we are working with.

As of the writing of this, this agency is under direct attack right now by the federal administration. No one can say with confidence at this time how the agency will act going forward with regards to queer and trans kid's rights—or if this agency will even exist. But historically, this is the next level when reporting unequal treatment in school.

Reaching Out to a National Civil Rights Organization

If you have exhausted these avenues and still have not had a satisfactory result, and queer and trans kids are continuing to be harassed or discriminated against at your school, contact a national organization like the ACLU. Increasingly, this may be the only recourse students have in states that are re-interpreting Title IX to exclude queer and trans kids.

Anyone can help coach a student in filing these kinds of complaints. Parents, friends, administrators. I have been asked to help advocate for kids who have been bullied in local schools but have never once succeeded in helping a kid stay motivated and courageous enough to file even an administrative complaint with the school. They end up getting disheartened in one way or another. In one case, the school outed the kid to the family and they ended up being homeless for a time. After that experience, they did everything in their power to avoid interacting with school administration. Other kids fail to see the potential benefit, either for themselves or the others that come after them. They feel the risk of speaking out is simply not worth it. Their strategy ends up being social isolation, homeschooling, or graduating as quickly as possible to escape the school and then, often, the area entirely.

Finding kids who are motivated and tenacious enough to take a stand is a rare gift. If you identify one, do everything in your power to cultivate their power. Ultimately, they are the voices that administrators pay attention to. For the most part.

Next-Level Visibility at School

There are many ways we can increase visibility and inclusion for queer kids, and thus safety and acceptance over time. Queer kids are most marginalized in cultures where they are invisible and silenced. This can be due to cultures of hatred and bullying which lead to kids self-censoring and hiding themselves (being in the closet). Or there can be structural ways in which we are made invisible and voiceless, like at a school that will not stock books with queer themes in the library or prohibits LGBTQ health education.

Giving space and visibility to queer voices, stories, and organizations can have a multitude of benefits. In my town, there are a few older high schools and one very new one. Students and teachers tell me that a homophobic and transphobic culture persists at the older schools, but at the new one queer students feel much more accepted and welcomed. This might be why queer kids regularly request to be transferred there. The new school also hosts a Pride Prom for students from all the area schools. None of the other schools have ever held a Pride Prom.

Why is the culture of the new school more accepting? I agree with one teacher's assessment, because the newer school was established with the latest anti-bullying policies and a culture of inclusion set by the administration at its founding.

The older schools required amendments to policies to ensure the protection of transgender students, for example, whereas the new school *started* with the most updated thinking on these matters.

Changing the culture at a school, like any large institution, takes years and decades of work. While I don't offer many quick answers, the next section will give you some ideas on ways to increase visibility and space for queer kids at your school, which invites participation that might have otherwise been avoided.

START A GSA

GSA—historically, an acronym for a "gay-straight alliance"—has recently been made over as a "gender and sexualities alliance." Whatever you take the letters to stand for, a GSA is a K-12 school-based club focused on supporting LGBTQ kids.

Like any club, any teacher can start one up, and a teacher must remain involved as club advisor for the club to continue throughout the years. Sadly, in the county I live in, I've watched GSA advisors, most often a queer-identified teacher, leave campus, and the students are left with a dissolved club when no one volunteers to take up the mantle.

You may be intimidated by the idea of founding or taking over advising a GSA club if you are cis and straight. But as we learned in 2024, the Governor of Minnesota and vice-presidential candidate, Tim Walz, a married, straight, cis white man, started one in the middle of America in 1999. It was easy for reporters to find former students and club members who praised him for this and were eager to share how his club changed their lives.

If your school doesn't have a GSA and there is no one else

interested in starting one, there is nothing stopping you from being that person. My suggestion to you would be to try to reach out to other GSA advisors in your surrounding area for advice. The other most important and overarching advice is to let the students lead. Ask the students what they would like to see. If the club just becomes a big socializing hour, then that's what's needed. If students have ideas for activities or actions, be a smart guide towards safe, inclusive, and ethical choices.

That's kind of it.

Administrators, how can you protect and support your GSAs? Can you shout them out in announcements or newsletters? Ask them if they would feel comfortable with that. Can you network and ask around if an advisor is retiring or leaving for another position and needs a successor?

GLSEN AND GSA NETWORK

GLSEN is a national organization supporting queer K-12 students and educators. GLSEN chapters organize local resource lists, connect GSA advisors, and sometimes hold community events. You may be able to find a chapter near you.

When I started a local chapter of GLSEN and got a group of GSA advisors together for a casual coffee, a profound thing happened. One of them shared that a large teachers association or local union regularly offered thousands of dollars in annual grants to GSAs. The money could be used for anything including saving. All you had to do was ask. This simple meeting, connection, and conversation unlocked thousands of dollars that were just waiting around for local clubs to ask for.

If there isn't a GLSEN chapter in your area, start one! Administrators, parents, students, former students, really anyone, can start, run, chair, or otherwise support a local chapter of GLSEN. You just need some spare time, the inclination to do some networking, and the ability to keep a database of local GSA advisors, presidents, and leaders of queer clubs at local colleges or universities. It can be a lot of upkeep because the people involved in these initiatives graduate, move on, and retire. But can you help?

I don't have personal experience with GSA Network, but I have heard great things about what they are doing lately. It could be a good idea to research starting a chapter with them as well!

PRIDE PROM

Some local GSAs in my area pool money together to hold a local Pride Prom open to any student in the county or neighboring counties. Pride Proms can be held on campus, where the usual prom is held, or in a separate location—wherever students feel most safe to openly be themselves. A Pride Prom will always be welcoming of gender non-conforming dress and any types of couples. They can feature fun and fanciful themes, drag performances, and DJs.

It's great if a Pride Prom is a team effort between multiple schools, local LGBTQ nonprofits, and other orgs that might have space and sound equipment to donate. Can you make these connections? This is a great job for an administrator, parent, or group of parents. Don't leave all the work to the GSAs themselves.

Create Inclusive Lesson Plans

Like I described in "Chapter 7: Create Visibility," stories about queer and trans lives are essential for the development of our identities. I did not know that I could transition to male until

I saw someone who did it. I did not know that we could be the heroes of our own, unique stories. Growing up, I thought that queerness had to remain hidden, as it seemed it was clearly unpalatable to most people. One job of a teacher, I might argue, is to show kids possibilities.

Queer people have made historical impacts in all subjects. No matter what you teach, you can find queer trailblazers to talk about, like:

- Alan Lay, transgender physician who pioneered using x-rays to screen for tuberculosis.

- Charley Parkhurst, transgender Gold Rush stagecoach driver.

- Amelio Robles Ávila, transgender veteran of the Mexican Revolution.

- Mary Oliver, lesbian poet who won the Pulitzer Prize and National Book Award.

- Audre Lorde, queer, feminist poet and civil rights activist.

- Alan Turing, father of computer science prosecuted and punished for being gay.

- James Baldwin, queer civil rights activist and author.

- Kiyoshi Kuromiya, co-founder of Gay Liberation Front and marijuana decriminalization activist.

- Harvey Milk, first openly gay person elected to public office in California who was assassinated.

Check out the website *Making Gay History* for lesson plans created by teachers. *Social Justice Books* is another great website that maintains queer-focused book lists by age group from school-aged kids to young adults, including banned books. There's a list of resources at the end of this book that might inspire you, too.

Next-level allies share resources and talk to their peers about why this is important. They stand up and speak out against book bans on queer stories. They highlight queer figures in history instead of burying them. Against all those who wish we would just be quiet and go away, they argue for our inclusion. They remind others that opening conversations in this way is the most effective key to creating a safe space where students are emboldened to participate honestly and authentically.

CHAPTER 12

NEXT–LEVEL MENTAL HEALTH PROFESSIONALS

Mental health professionals, like social workers, therapists, psychiatrists, nurses, techs, and nurse practitioners next-level educate themselves. I have had some professional experience working as a mental health case manager in a large health clinic and as a nurse in a locked psychiatric facility. The mental health-specific training I received was minimal, and, at the time, I did not receive any LGBTQ-specific training. Times have changed and professionals in this field may be exposed to more specific job training than I was.

Regardless, there are numerous, free opportunities to learn how to better serve LGBTQ people and become a next-level mental health professional. One is the National LGBTQIA+ Health Education Center from the Fenway Institute in Boston. Their website offers hundreds of free learning resources; sort by "behavioral health" to find modules focused on the LGBTQ experience of navigating mental health challenges.

This chapter is not a substitute for the above work. Rather, here I will outline specific concerns a lot of queer people have when interacting with mental health professionals. I will also show you a few concrete things you can do to help the queers in your community. And I'll end with an absolutely crucial step that all mental health providers who call themselves LGBTQ-serving must do. I don't operate with a lot of absolutes, but this is one of them.

Don't Advertise What You Can't Offer

Have you marked yourself as "LGBTQ" competent on *Psychology Today,* on insurance search tools, or somewhere else you are listed? What does that mean to you?

I'd encourage you to consider this question deeply if you haven't already. Imagine a client asking you what exactly you are going to offer them as an LGBTQ person? What kind of specialty education have you had on the subject? What specific expertise can you offer?

If you don't have a ready answer—if you only marked yourself that way because you are not a hateful person—I'd encourage you to reconsider your marker. I'll be honest, among the LGBTQ community it is a bit of a cultural trope at this point. When speaking to a friend who is shopping for a therapist or has recently signed on with a new one, we ask are they *really* LGBTQ competent? With a knowing wink. Or did they mark themselves that way without having a clue about our specific experiences and needs?

I would hate to discourage a mental health provider from helping LGBTQ people—I hope you know that is opposite the intention of this book! But at the same time, being an ally to

LGBTQ people as a mental health provider requires a little something extra. As I say in the Introduction to this book, being an ally is more than just an intention and an absence of hate. It is action.

To me, a mental health provider who is truly LGBTQ-competent is either queer or trans themselves or has had enough successful interactions with and positive reviews from queer and trans clients that they can confidently state that they have specific expertise in the subject. They usually have also sought out specific training.

Next-level LGBTQ-competent mental health providers have also done one or more of the following: made a list of community resources, started a support group, and learned about writing letters of support for trans people.

COMMUNITY RESOURCES: MAKE A LIST

Gather a resource list for your clients that includes the hyperlocal—not just the national. I'm talking about food resources, housing, legal advocacy, trans and queer specific healthcare organizations or clinics, electrolysis clinics (required for many trans people before surgery), clothing resources, LGBTQ centers and events, LGBTQ-specific support groups, recovery groups and programs, NAMI chapters, and more. Share this in your office and on your website.

START A SUPPORT GROUP

Mental health practitioners are generally trained in facilitating support groups. Are there support groups existing already at LGBTQ centers in your area? Ask them if they could use you as a volunteer to act as an alternate or substitute. As you know, it is best to have similarly identified peers facilitating support groups. But it can be difficult to find and retain facilitators, and there might be opportunities for you to step in as a substitute in emergencies. If your local LGBTQ center does not have any existing support groups, ask if you might be of service in starting some, maybe you can use your expertise to train facilitators.

If there are no LGBTQ-focused support groups or organizations in your area, start one. Host a meetup or social event. Start somewhere. Do you work for a county behavioral health system? Great place to start an LGBTQ support group. Is your expertise in substance use treatment? Can you identify some good facilitators and make space for queer recovery groups?

Write Letters of Support for Trans People

Trans people need a letter of support from a mental health professional before seeking gender-affirming care. In some places, it's required to start hormones. In others, it's only required before surgery. Every community needs more competent professionals who can offer this service. In my rural area, it has been a constant struggle to identify providers at the blessed intersection of being able to write letters supporting trans people in their medical transition and who accept the local Medicaid or low-income insurance. Or Medicare! These are the angels of their local trans and LGBTQ community, the super-allies.

To me, there are few more impactful ways that straight folks can ally themselves with queer justice. You can learn how to perform this service online for free at the National LGBTQIA+ Health Education Center's website. If you ultimately decide that you aren't comfortable being the person who writes letters of support for transgender people, find the person or agency in your community who does, so you can refer your clients there when needed.

I don't operate in a lot of absolutes. But if you are a mental healthcare provider who doesn't provide letters of support for transgender people and doesn't know to whom you can refer transgender people for these letters then you are not yet a next-level ally. And you probably shouldn't mark yourself as LGBTQ-competent or serving on listing sites.

Knowing where to refer people for the services they need is the bare minimum for allies in this profession. Trans folks are the most vulnerable among us and need that letter to start living their lives.

CHAPTER 13

NEXT–LEVEL MEDICAL PROFESSIONALS

This chapter will give an extremely brief overview of some considerations that health professionals can think about in their practice. Whether you are an EMT, paramedic, medical assistant, nurse, physician's assistant, or medical doctor, you come across LGBTQ folks in your practice every day. In 2023, the Williams Institute estimated that about 5% of Americans are LGBTQ.[24] Therefore, if you are not aware of LGBTQ clients in your practice, that means you have not developed a close and trusting relationship with them—one in which they have felt comfortable to be open and honest with you about their life and their loved ones.

I would challenge you to consider how this might affect the care that you are giving them. Can you provide sexual health and family planning that makes sense for them? And if they don't feel comfortable sharing about their relationship or their

---

24 Andrew R. Flores and Kerith J. Conron, "Adult LGBT Population in the United States," UCLA School of Law Williams Institute, 2023, https://williamsinstitute.law.ucla.edu/wp-content/uploads/LGBT-Adult-US-Pop-Dec-2023.pdf.

loved ones with you, what else might they be uncomfortable opening up about?

I've been a registered nurse for the past ten years. I've worked with hundreds of trans patients at Santa Rosa Community Health and as a facilitator of a support group for trans and non-binary people in a rural area that lacks specialist providers. I'm also a queer and transgender patient myself. Needless to say, I have a lot of opinions on this subject.

It would be impossible to build a step-by-step guide to caring for all queer and transgender folks, not only because queer people are not a monolith, but also because there are so many different roles that healthcare providers fill. That said, I would like to share some advice and experiences that might help you become a next-level medical professional.

Sexual Health History

Every provider evolves their own, natural way of taking a sexual health history. This is usually based on heteronormative concerns like asking binary questions about relationship status or focusing only on the act of cis people making babies and the assorted concerns therein.

I'll make it as succinct as I can. Remove assumptions. Queer culture is growing and evolving before our eyes. You and I will never attain "cultural competency." The landscape moves too fast. That is why the preferred terms now are cultural sensitivity, and *cultural humility.*

Providers with cultural humility ask the most open of open-ended questions when first meeting a client. Don't ask me if I am gay or lesbian. Don't put inaccurate words in your client's mouth. Ask me if I am comfortable sharing with you about how

I identify regarding my sexuality and gender. If there is hesitation, move on and return to this later, after trust has been built.

Know that many queer and trans people avoid gendered cancer screenings due to being uncomfortable with pelvic exams. Don't gloss over and ignore this question in mutual discomfort. Let your client know why screenings are important and ask how you can be supportive throughout the process. Invite them to talk about any fears. Listen for and mirror language they use for their own body parts. Don't assume anything about queer or transgender people's genitals; ask them how they refer to the parts they have.

Don't Make the Client Educate You

This might seem like a paradox at first glance. On the one hand, yes, we have to be open when initially meeting our clients in order for them to be able to explain themselves accurately and in the ways they feel comfortable. Remember don't make assumptions. But once you have a baseline understanding about how your client identifies, be aware of relying too much on the LGBTQ person to alert you to everything they need.

If you don't have experience with queer or trans patients and you suddenly find yourself with one, reach out to colleagues for help. Up until recently, transgender care was incredibly hard to find. This forced trans people to learn about the medicine they need and describe to a willing provider how to prescribe it. You can do better than that. You can also research and learn how to best support queer and trans patients; a good place to start is the National LGBTQIA+ Health Education Center. There you can deepen your knowledge about our unique needs and life experiences and bring that next-level awareness to your practice.

Prevent HIV

Did you know that you can prevent HIV extremely effectively with a once-daily pill? Every single time I speak to a group of medical providers or students, I make sure to mention this because there are still people who don't know. Help me spread this information. Prescribe PrEP, PEP, and DoxyPEP. Make sure you know where to refer folks for the MPOX vaccine. Unfamiliar with these? Look them up.

Prescribe Trans Care

Transgender care, essentially hormone replacement therapy (HRT), is among the safest areas of care to work in. Consider adding this to your practice if you are a primary care provider or endocrinologist. The most widely used and regarded guidelines for transgender care are from the University of California at San Francisco (UCSF) and the Fenway Institute in Boston. Look them up. Questions? Navigate to the Fenway Institute's National LGBTQIA+ Health Education Center's website.

Community Partnerships

Are you already prescribing trans care, HIV care, or HIV prevention? Then make sure you are allied with your local LGBTQ-serving organizations so they know how to refer clients to you. (And thank you.)

The medical providers in my rural area are, in the words of their clients, singular pillars holding up our entire community. Recently, I've been holding panel discussions with local trans patients and queer Hmong folks for medical students at UCSF. I was so touched when one of the participants described our sole, local, trans medicine prescriber as that pillar. This straight cis super-ally essentially provides almost all of the primary care for the entire trans community in our small town of Merced. The panel participant described the fear and horror they feel at the thought of her ever leaving the area, which could certainly happen. We live in a low-income area, designated as a health professional shortage area by the state. Anyone who has lived here for some amount of time has had a medical provider move away for better opportunities. It is devilishly hard to get any kind of specialty care here, with long waiting lists for everyone from a pulmonologist to an orthopedist.

What will we do if our provider of transgender care leaves? Basically, another super-ally or group of allies will have to be willing to step in to prescribe care for us remotely. Or we will be forced to seek out our own primary care providers and individually lobby and educate them into providing us the care we need to live. Another panel participant illustrated it brilliantly: If you go to the doctor because you are having heart trouble, you can be reasonably sure they will, at the very least, believe you, and be able to direct you to the care you need. But we can't count on that when seeking trans care.

Medical professionals who are next-level allies help trans folks get the care they need at any point in the cycle of care. That means everyone—from the intake worker in the emergency department to the phlebotomist drawing blood to the RN in the hospital—has the opportunity to step up.

Chapter 14

NEXT-LEVEL JUSTICE AND LEGAL PROFESSIONALS

Law enforcement is meant to serve and protect all people and ensure equal protection under the law. If you work in local policing, probation, law, immigration, or the National Guard or armed forces, you already know that it is your duty to apply the law to everyone equally. However, queer people throughout history know that we have been treated differently, and that seeps into the perception many of us have of people working in these fields. To prove our fears are unfounded you have to be next-level.

In this chapter, I hope to illuminate and illustrate some places where the justice system currently fails queer people so that you can find and identify gaps that affect the communities you serve. But I think all allies should study these stories because so many of us know victims of crime and abuse and have loved ones who have been affected by the justice system. I'm sharing Beth's and Tony's stories because allies need to be armed with real stories so they can advocate for better and more equal protections for all. For more stories about queer and trans people in the justice system visit The Marshall Project.[25]

BETH'S STORY

In March of 2021, transgender woman Beth (pseudonym) was arrested in Merced, California after defending herself from a violent attack. Beth is a good friend of mine who I let stay at my house for a while when she was experiencing homelessness. She was eager to share her story, though it was very difficult for her to tell, and it took a year or two of recovery for her to feel able to share it. She feels strongly that stories of police abuse be shared widely so she gave me permission to share this.

I was arrested without explanation. My Miranda rights were not read. I was taken to the Merced County Sheriff's Office on M Street and put into a holding cell. I went through the intake process and was left in the holding cell for several hours.

In the middle of the night at some point, I was transferred to Sandy Mush whereupon I was put into another cell. Four officers came into my cell: two male officers and two female officers. Their manner was intimidating: one was standing at the door while the other three entered my cell. One of the female officers stated that they needed to see my private parts. They didn't say why or give any reason. They stated that I could choose to comply or they would be forced to

---

25 "What Being Trans in Prison Is Really Like" is an excellent piece of reporting by Beth Schwartzapfel from 2024 where several trans women share stories of being raped by staff and having their heads forcibly shaved. https://www.themarshallproject.org/2024/04/26/trans-prison-voices-gender-essay.

Trans Women Are Women

Does what happened to Beth happen to most women when they are incarcerated? If not, why not? How can you ensure that transgender people are protected from forced genital inspections where you work? Is it in written policy? Do staff receive training that discusses this specifically?

As of this writing in 2025, the Department of Justice has removed statistics about transgender people and crime from its website. However, this does not remove the truth that trans women are much more likely to be *victims* of sexual abuse in prison than perpetrators. This was captured from the removed Department of Justice site via the Wayback Machine:[26]

Fifteen percent of transgender individuals report being sexually assaulted while in police custody or jail, which more than doubles (32 percent) for African-American transgender people. Five to nine percent of

---

26 U.S. Department of Justice: Office for Victims Of Crime, "Responding to Transgender Victims of Sexual Assault," accessed February 22, 2026, https://web.archive.org/web/20250117162658/https://ovc.ojp.gov/sites/g/files/xyckuh226/files/pubs/forge/sexual_numbers.html.

transgender survivors were sexually assaulted by police officers. Another 10 percent were assaulted by health care professionals.

The Bureau of Prisons *Transgender Offender Manual* from 2017 recommends housing by gender identity when safe and appropriate. That means trans women are women and should be housed with women by default, making exceptions only for the most concerning of violent offenders. Taking this approach also removes the need to inspect people's genitals which is humiliating and unnecessary.

This is echoed in PREA (Prison Rape Elimination Act) Standard 115.42(e)[27] which states, "A transgender or intersex inmate's own views with respect to his or her own safety shall be given serious consideration."

Protecting the safety of incarcerated trans women by housing them with women is codified in California law. But not everywhere. What can you do to protect incarcerated trans men and women where you are?

> ## TONY'S STORY
> Tony (pseudonym), a gay man, suffered a decade of increasing domestic violence at the hands of his partner of twenty-five years. He didn't get the results he needed from the justice system until he happened to befriend his city's mayor who spoke to the district attorney on his behalf. The mayor asked why a decade of reported violence had never ended up with a felony conviction? A felony conviction is what Tony needed in order to get permanent protection and his abuser out of the house.

27 National PREA Resource Center, "PREA Standards," accessed February 22, 2026, https://www.prearesourcecenter.org/standard/115-42.

Tony and I both wanted to have his story in his own words in these pages. Ultimately, though, it was too hard for him to sit down and write, or tell me, the whole story chronologically. It is too fresh right now—he only recently was able to find safety for himself. Tony has been my friend for fifteen years, though, and he consented to have me summarize what happened to the best of my ability.

Tony was in this domestic partnership (which started way before gay marriage was legalized) for more than twenty-five years. For the final decade, though, he was emotionally and physically abused by his stronger partner, as Tony suffered several debilitating health conditions that caused seizures and left him weak and less able to defend himself.

Tony says that friends have told him that he would have never had to suffer so long if he had been in a heterosexual partnership. Why? He explained that he felt that every time he called the cops they treated the situation "like two guys having a fistfight in a bar." He says he was never seen as the victim even though he was the only one with injuries.

Everyone Can Experience Domestic Violence

As next-level allies, we need to understand that studies continue to confirm that LGBTQ people experience disproportionate rates of domestic violence. Complicating matters, most domestic violence shelters around the county only admit women and children so it can be more difficult for a man to leave an abusive home.

What kind of resources can you point LGBTQ couples to in

your area? Are there shelters and victim services organizations that serve people of all genders? If not, why not? What can you do to advocate for this or create alternatives?

Next-level allies who work in or closely with the justice system have a lot of work to do, and lots of hard conversations to have with those they work with. What can you do to better ensure equity and safety for all the people you serve? Can you advocate for LGBTQ cultural competency training? Next-level organizations partner with local LGBTQ organizations who can provide this training.

A victim support organization in my community hosts a National Crime Victim's Rights Week event where local organizations can showcase and network to strengthen their web of interconnected services. This includes LGBTQ organizations, victim support groups, homeless services groups, and more. Featured speakers include not only government and law enforcement officials, but victims of crime including local transgender people. Brainstorming about how you can craft an event where the most marginalized of us feel invited to participate is next-level ally work, and helps keep everyone safer.

CHAPTER 15

NEXT-LEVEL FAMILIES

We don't have to have positions of power like those listed in the last chapters to make a difference. Being champions of queer justice within our own families can be a full time job—or even a lifetime's work. If family members are steeped in hateful and exclusionary cultures, you likely won't make a difference overnight.

In this chapter, I'll summarize a few conversational tactics that you can use in commonly-encountered exchanges with family members who aren't yet open to the reality of LGBTQ people being active participants in society.[28]

Talking to Family

In order to begin to foster radical empathy within your cis-

---

28 Steven T. Collis' pretty excellent *Habits of a Peacemaker* (you can skip over the strange diatribe about critical social theories) gives a thorough breakdown of the conversational habits required, and the mindset needed, to start slowly chipping away at the hateful ideas that others have. He cautions that emotional escalation is rarely helpful and details strategies that help us dismantle the unfounded fears of LGBTQ people that people have.

hetero family, it's necessary to start from a place of empathy for your family's life experience. If they grew up in the middle of the last century (1950s and 60s), they were raised with negative stereotypes, customs, and norms about queer people. They grew up in a time where it was literally illegal to be gay in most parts of the world. They might see hiding queerness as just a natural feature of society. They might have all sorts of feelings about this, but if they don't have queer people in their lives, it will be mostly subconscious and unexamined. These ideas might be difficult to uncover and address. This takes time (patience), skill, and tact.

If you start by telling people they're wrong, it seldom moves the needle. Rather, we have to get them comfortable with exploring the reasons why they hold their outdated views. These reasons can be where they came from or how those views are perpetuated by what they see around them today.

Sometimes families can have ways of speaking that are homophobic or transphobic, but they might not recognize it as such. They might say, "Well, that was just a joke." You could take this opportunity to explain to them why this kind of joke could be hurtful to some people they might know or point out that it is not helpful to perpetuate negative stereotypes about people. Perhaps you can explain that it is not a good example to set for others, especially if there are children present. You can explain, "Stereotypes aren't true about everybody, are they?" Framing the issue as part of a bigger cultural shift towards understanding and kindness can be a good tactic. Play on their desires to teach their children about fairness.

If your folks or kin say something homophobic, transphobic, or otherwise unnecessarily exclusionary, ask them why they feel that way. You may be surprised with what you find. It might end up being a falsehood that is surprisingly easy to dismantle.

PFLAG

I don't have personal experience with PFLAG as there is no local chapter in my area. But my understanding is that PFLAG creates spaces and opportunities for families to have conversations about how best to support their queer family members. It could be a worthwhile resource to tap into in your area. Whether you are queer yourself, or have queer colleagues, students, or clients who are experiencing family conflict, PFLAG might be able to help either the queer person or the family members—whomever is ready to accept help.

No PFLAG chapter in your area? Start one!

Talking to Children

There is simply no reason for me to overlap much with Lindz Amer and their wonderful book *Rainbow Parenting*. There, they talk at length, and with great insight, experience, and expertise, about talking to kids about queerness. Their book provides profound insights for teachers, school administrators, GSA leaders, parents, foster parents, grandparents, aunties, uncles, daycare staff, pediatricians, mental health professionals, and really, anyone who ever interacts with kids.

Besides advising you to pick up this book, I'll just summarize some key points:

- Combat hypersexualization by reminding everyone that queer identities aren't just about sex: they are about love, families, marriage.

- Don't treat queerness as something strange or something to keep hidden. Rather explain situations in simple terms appropriate for the child's developmental age—"Yes, Juan and Dave are married, that's normal" or "Anyone can wear makeup and nail polish."

- Age-appropriate education about bodies, consent, and sex is *abuse prevention* because it gives kids the language tools to protect their bodies, and it removes the stigma about talking about queer identities.

- Teaching body language, body consent, and body kindness starts to dismantle the culture abusers and bullies thrive in. Abusers prey on ignorance and secrecy.

Basically, normalize queerness. This is appropriate whether your kid is queer or straight. It is never too early to build empathy by consuming media with queer content: picture books, YA novels, graphic novels, shows, and movies. There is more and more queer media available everyday. Let it become a natural part of the language of your home. Don't perpetuate the notion that we ought to be hidden from view, are taboo, or disgusting.

CHAPTER 16

NEXT-LEVEL EDUCATION FOR YOURSELF AND OTHERS

I can't tell you what you need to educate yourself on. I don't know you, where you live, what your circumstances are, or what your society and culture are like. All these things are deeply localized. What works for one person in one part of the world might not work for someone in another part of the world at this particular time. I wish the globe was in unison on striving to be more conscious, but sadly, we know this is not the case.

A key to educating yourself is to be interested in what you're learning. Did you absorb every class you took in school? Of course not. No one did. No one will learn something just because they are told to, they have to be deeply interested in it and follow it themselves. So next-level educate yourself on the topics that interest you and are relevant to you and your local community.

I hope that if you've read this far in this book, you've come across topics that are new to you and you want to know more about. Maybe the chapters on political organizing, marching, volunteering, and making a fuss piqued your curiosity. If so, read up about the history of queer organizing. (There isn't a huge amount of titles on the subject but they are out there and more come out every year.) Or delve into the fascinating history of the intersection of labor organizing and the anarchist movement embodied in Emma Goldman. Or the Vietnam era protests, the Tiananmen Square Massacre, the history and art of ACT UP. See how the legends did it. All efforts at radical organizing and protest are applicable to this work, and just plain inspiring.

This chapter shares some ways to deepen your own education and move you closer to becoming a next-level ally.

Get a Library Card

Get a library card. Your library card gives you access to tons of print resources and multiple media apps with free ebooks, audiobooks, and movies to stream. (Also, your card shows your support for your local library in real numbers that matter to the government, which helps protect them against local efforts to privatize or defund them.) Check out queer-focused titles, even if you only skim or get partway through them. This also numerically proves community interest in queer titles ensuring your library continues to stock them and make them available to everyone.

If you're artistically inclined, seek out books about the history of political propaganda posters, of resistance, of revolutionary street art, or zines. Better yet, learn how to make zines and then hold a zine making event at your local library, queer center, indie bookshop, or cafe.

Take a Class

Maybe you're interested in the intersection of racism, feminism, queer justice, and Black Lives Matter? If so, I highly suggest you take a sociology class at your local community college. This might sound like a very boring prospect. But I, for one, learned so many interesting facts that I use to this day from these kinds of classes. If there is an option for you that highlights racial and ethnic injustice or gender politics, so much the better. Your talking points go way up with this, trust me.

Read Queer Stories and History

Maybe you have trans friends and want to be more informed about what they are going through with things like hormones and surgeries. I hope I don't need to remind you that asking your friends to explain all the technical ins and outs of surgeries and other ways to medically transition is not necessarily the most strategic move. It is your job now to educate yourself on the medical terminology that your friends may be using. But where to start?

There is actually a whole lot of great literature coming out on trans medicine and identity though not all of it is widely available or mainstream. Some great places to find these resources are zine or alternative press expos and festivals. DIY comics and zines are having a renaissance, or maybe a golden age, and there are lots of queer and trans voices telling incredible stories in graphic novels and small pamphlets and books. Ask your local booksellers or comic book shops if they can recommend any LGBTQ-specific titles. And have a look at the brief but spectacular "Resources" section at the end of this book for online collections of queer and trans stories—100s of them—free to browse from projects like *StoryCorps* and *OutHistory*.

Remember that in the end, your goal is to explain these topics, these histories, and these political realities to others in the spirit of a radical empathy exercise. You are not learning this just for fun or curiosity. You are learning these things so that queer and trans people do not have to do all the organizing, explaining, educating, and putting themselves out there and on the line. That is your job now.

Visualizing yourself explaining the topic that you're learning about is a great way to know that you've got the content

down. Better yet, go ahead and really explain it to someone. I did this a lot in nursing school. I would sit a friend down and say, "OK. I am going to explain how cells in the body process sugar to you because I am studying it right now and this is a good way to see if I understand it correctly." Often, I would come to a gap in my knowledge and realize it was something that I had to read more about.

Start a Book Club

Since talking it out with someone is an invaluable tool for learning, maybe start a book club? You and a few friends (or just one!) agree to read a book together about they/them pronouns, queer justice, or anything else. It can be a small book or zine; it doesn't have to be a serious research endeavor. Make it fun! This is a great way to start getting out of our bubbles, too. Invite a work friend. A neighbor. Fellow parents. Teachers.

If you are brave, make an ad or advertise your club on a small index card and pin it to the bulletin board of your local cafe. You might be surprised who ends up expressing interest in the club once you put it out there.

Schedule a monthly meetup. Hold yourselves accountable for talking about the cool text you just read and your plans to implement the lessons you've taken from it. Or maybe it doesn't have explicit lessons in it. Maybe it is a comedy or a novel. Still, discuss what your takeaways are. Talk about:

- How the queer characters struggled with things that you've never had to.

- A radically different perspective or take on something that you've never considered.

- How queer characters found solace and support.

- How you can translate these revelations into action in your own community or family.

If you are stuck on what book to choose, go to your local bookstore and see what recommendations their staff might have. Or let me recommend a natural place to start: Maia Kobabe's graphic novel, *Genderqueer.* Discuss why it was the most banned book of 2023.[29]

There are lots of professions that require a commitment to lifelong learning, not only in order to remain relevant and marketable, but to continue to provide the highest level of service possible. In the same way, next-level allies know that their learning is never finished, especially in these exciting times when more and more queer people are coming out, sharing their stories, and reimagining the language around gender and sexuality in real time. For me, I find this kind of perpetual cycle of learning, questioning, and then learning more things fun. Next-level allies figure out how to make the learning process enjoyable and accessible, they engage others and inspire people to learn to be better to everyone.

____

29 "Top 10 and Frequently Challenged Books Archive," American Library Association, accessed February 6, 2026, https://www.ala.org/bbooks/frequentlychallengedbooks/top10/archive.

CONCLUSION

Next-level allies move. They act. They create. They read books, yes, but then they discuss. They post. They protest. They train. They implement. They organize. The essential difference between a true ally and a mere well-wisher is *action*.

I have known so many next-level allies. The public health educator who reached out to my transgender support group and offered to give talks on stress management which ended up being super popular. The teacher who organizes and coaches groups of students on how to show up and speak out against hate at school board meetings. And there are so many next-level allies who I will never meet. Tim Walz who started a GSA in 1999. The librarians who put time and effort into making awesome displays for Pride month and Banned Books Week. Parents who move across the country so their child can continue to access gender-affirming care after it was banned in their home state. The thousands of people who help by writing public comments against proposed hateful legislation. People who distribute naloxone (Narcan) and food and clothing free of charge and without judgement. And some next-level allies are among the closest people to me like my parents who eventually learned how to use my new name and pronouns. It took years, and we both ran out of patience at times, but we got through it. Now, they go to Pride demonstrations and the Trans March in San Francisco by themselves if I am not around.

Mom and I had an interesting conversation recently. She is now in the habit of almost always wearing something with rainbow colors or a trans flag—be it homemade, crocheted flowers on her hat band or a bracelet or socks. She told me about how she notices that conversations definitely change when she is wearing these things. She notices that people notice. She says that people who she has previously heard engaging in ugly discussions about anything—trans people, immigrants, the Russian invasion of Ukraine—now just avoid her altogether. Which she thinks is great! And at the same time, she reports it definitely opens up conversations that may have not otherwise happened—often with other parents of queer kids; conversations that can be so meaningful as knowledge and perspectives are shared. In her words, "It matters."

What will you do? How will you speak up—and follow through—for change? I couldn't begin to count the number of suggestions I have given at work, at my city council, or any number of organizations I've interacted with over the years that were never acted on. Honestly, in my personal and professional experience changes aren't often made until someone has been an absolute pest about it. Will you continue to follow up, over years if necessary, to see a change through in your organization? Will you make it part of your elevator speech, peppering those around you with your great ideas for change and gathering support along the way?

If your queer book club doesn't end up forming, will you pivot and try something else? Will you be creative with your unique situation? If you are straight and cis, will you go to your local queer organizations and ask them what it is *they* need? Will you partner with them on projects and share resources, space, and media reach? Will you put queer and trans voices in positions of power? Will you give them platforms? Air time? Encouragement?

Yes! You will! Because you are a next-level ally. You are educated about queer history and therefore make clear, practical arguments to the people around you for why queer people need visibility and protection, and you give concrete examples. You create safe spaces where people feel comfortable being open about who they are. You are a champion of your queer friends because you have the confidence to stand up for them when it makes sense and the sense to make space for them when it's their time to shine. You are working to make your corner of the world a safer and more colorful place. And you are committed to a lifelong learning practice—of a consistent diet of queer and trans stories, awareness of the news, policies, and politics that affect us—and you explain on our behalf why all of this is so very important.

NEXT-LEVEL RESOURCES

Here are some books, websites, archives, and zines that can help you deepen your next-level allyship even more. It is by no means an exhaustive list, but it is a great place to start.

Advocacy and Activism

- *Somebody Should Do Something: How Anyone Can Help Create Social Change* by Michael Brownstein, Alex Madva, and Daniel Kelly (The MIT Press, 2025)

On Whistleblowing

- *Win the Inside Game: How to Move From Surviving to Thriving, and Free Yourself Up to Perform* by Steve Magness (Harper Collins, 2025)

Making Charged Conversations More Productive

- *Habits of a Peacemaker: 10 Habits to Change Our Potentially Toxic Conversations into Healthy Dialogues* by Steven T. Collis (Shadow Mountain, 2024)

General LGBTQ Knowledge

- *The ABC's of LGBT+* by Ash Hardell (Mango Media Inc., 2016)
- *A Quick & Easy Guide to They/Them Pronouns* by Archie

Bongiovanni and Tristan Jimerson (Oni Press, 2018)
- *A Quick & Easy Guide to Queer & Trans Identities* by Mady G. and Jules Zuckerberg (Oni Press, 2019)
- *A Quick & Easy Guide to Asexuality* by Molly Muldoon and Will Hernandez (Oni Press, 2022)
- *A Quick & Easy Guide to Coming Out* by Kristin Russo and Ravi Teixeira (Oni Press, 2024)

Caring for Queer Kids
- *Rainbow Parenting: Your Guide to Raising Queer Kids and Their Allies* by Lindz Amer (St. Martin's Publishing Group, 2023)
- *I Love My Queer Kid: A Workbook to Affirm and Support Your LGBTQ+ Child Or Teen* by Marc Campbell (Microcosm Publishing, 2023)

Books for Teachers
- *Culturally Responsive Teaching and the Brain: Promoting Authentic Engagement and Rigor Among Culturally and Linguistically Diverse Students* by Zaretta Hammond (Corwin, 2014)
- *Understanding and Teaching: U.S. Lesbian, Gay, Bisexual, and Transgender History* edited by Leila J. Rupp and Susan K. Freeman (University of Wisconsin Press, 2017)
- *One Teacher in Ten in the New Millennium: LGBT Educators Speak Out About What's Gotten Better . . . and What Hasn't* by Kevin Jennings (Beacon Press, 2015)
- *Teaching the Teachers: LGBTQ Issues in Teacher Education* by Cathy A. R. Brant and Lara M. Willox (Information Age Publishing, 2020)
- *Teaching, Affirming, and Recognizing Trans and Gender Creative Youth* edited by sj Miller (Palgrave Macmillan, 2016)

- *Critical Democratic Education and LGBTQ-Inclusive Curriculum: Opportunities and Constraints* by Steven Camicia (Routledge, 2016)

Queer History for Young Adults

- *Queer, There, and Everywhere: 27 People Who Changed the World* by Sarah Prager and illustrated by Zoe More O'Ferrall (Harper Collins, 2023)
- *Queer: A Graphic History* by Meg-John Barker and Jules Scheele (Icon Books, 2016)
- *A Queer History of the United States For Young People* by Michael Bronski, adapted by Richie Chevat (Beacon Press, 2019)

Queer Organizing History

- *The Stonewall Reader* edited by The New York Public Library and Jason Baumann (Penguin Classics, 2019)
- *Generation Queer: Stories of Youth Organizers, Artists, and Educators* by Kimm Topping (Lee & Low Books, 2025)
- ACT UP Oral History Project (https://www.actuporalhistory.org/)

The Justice System

- *Queer (In)Justice: The Criminalization of LGBT People in the United States* by Joey L. Mogul, Andrea J. Ritchie, and Kay Whitlock (Beacon Press, 2012)

Books for Mental Health Professionals

- *Queering Your Therapy Practice* by Julie Tilsen (Routledge, 2021)
- *The Modern Clinician's Guide to Working with LGBTQ+ Clients: The Inclusive Psychotherapist* by Margaret Nichols (Routledge, 2020)
- *Pocket Guide to LGBTQ Mental Health: Understanding*

the Spectrum of Gender and Sexuality by Petros Levounis and Eric Yarbrough (American Psychiatric Association Publishing, 2020)

- *A Clinician's Guide to Gender-Affirming Care: Working with Transgender and Gender Nonconforming Clients* by Sand C. Chang, Anneliese A. Singh, and lore m. dickey (Context Press, 2018)

Continuing Education (CE) for Health and Mental Health Professionals

- National LGBTQIA+ Health Education Center (https://www.lgbtqiahealtheducation.org/)

Personal Queer and Trans Stories

- Making Gay History (https://makinggayhistory.org/)
- NYC Trans Oral History Project (https://nyctransoralhistory.org/)
- OutHistory (https://outhistory.org/)
- StoryCorps LGBTQ Archives (https://storycorps.org/theme/lgbtq/)

GLOSSARY

Aromantic: Someone who does not experience romantic attraction. Recently adopted as falling under the LGBTQ flag as an identity minority.

Asexual: Someone who does not experience sexual attraction. Recently adopted as falling under the LGBTQ flag as a sexual identity minority.

Bisexual: Term for someone sexually attracted to multiple genders. Some argue that since the term itself suggests a gender binary (bi), now seen as inaccurate (there are many gender identities), that those also attracted to trans and non-binary identities should therefore use the terms omnisexual or pansexual. Older people having identified as bisexual for decades may not choose to switch their identity. Others argue that the term bisexual doesn't necessarily exclude trans and non-binary identities and is interchangeable with pansexual and omnisexual. It's a great example of language and culture continuing to evolve in real time.

Cis: Short for cisgender. Someone who has never considered altering their gender identity or presentation from the one assigned at birth.

Cis-het, cisgender hetoronormative, normative, straight and cis: Different ways to describe people who are not LGBTQ.

Crossdressing and drag: Dressing in a gender non-conforming way regardless of personal gender identity (can be performed by both trans and cis people).

DEI: Acronym for diversity, equity and inclusion. Has become widely adopted as a catch-all term for programming that uplifts minority voices and justice including Black and queer justice.

Demisexual: Demisexual people require a strong emotional bond before developing sexual attraction.

DIY: Do-it-yourself. An ethic of creating and constructing things by hand.

Drag king: A woman or non-binary person performing or dressing as a man. This is separate from personal identity: they may or may not personally identify as trans.

Drag queen: A man or non-binary person performing or dressing as a woman. This is separate from personal identity: they may or may not personally identify as trans.

Gay: Traditionally only used to describe men who love men. Claimed now by many younger people as an umbrella term with the same meaning and usage as "queer" and "LGBTQ."

Gender-affirming care: This is an umbrella term for medical or mental healthcare that affirms the patient's stated gender identity. This means supportive talk therapy, recommendations about non-invasive devices like chest binders, puberty-blocking/delaying therapy, hormone therapy including hormone suppression, and surgical interventions. A person receiving any one or more of these examples is receiving gender-affirming care: not all interventions are required or desired by everybody.

Gender identity: Your gender identity is how you feel about your own gender. Cisgender people have no conflict with their gender identity. Trans people feel in conflict with the gender assigned to them. Everyone has a gender identity. For cis people, your gender identity is male or female. For trans and non-binary people, there can be some nuance.

Graysexual: A term for the spectrum that lies between asexual and sexual. Includes identities like asexual, aromantic, and demisexual.

LGBTQ: Acronym for lesbian, gay, bisexual, transgender, and queer or questioning. Used primarily as an umbrella term encompassing all people who are not cisgender and straight. Academically, the most widely used and accepted term for this.

Non-binary: Umbrella term for people with a gender identity that does not conform to the binary idea of gender as being either male or female. Non-binary people can identify as either cis or trans. Non-binary people won't necessarily conform to what your idea of an androgynous look is. Some non-binary people choose transgender medical procedures and treatments but others do not.

Omnisexual or Pansexual: Terms describing someone attracted to all genders or attracted to qualities other than gender. Omnisexual was coined in the 1990s and is less used today. Pansexual came into use more recently and is the most widely used term. Historically speaking, these are newer terms for "bisexual" that some argue are more inclusive and encompassing of all genders.

Out (someone): To out someone, outing someone, or coming out is when an LGBTQ person's sexual or gender identity is revealed. This can happen consensually or non-consensually, at the initiation of the LGBTQ person or initiated by someone else in conversation, print, or otherwise.

Polyamory: The practice of having romantic and/or sexual relationships with multiple people. Some argue this sexual identity should fall under the LGBTQ flag as a signal of solidarity among marginalized sexual identities.

Queer: Umbrella term encompassing all LGBTQ identities and more. Anyone who is not both heterosexual *and* cisgender. Historically used as a slur, now widely reclaimed by the LGBTQ community as a positive identity. Use with caution in front of older audiences. More casual than LGBTQ, but also becoming more academically accepted as time goes on.

Questioning: Someone who is in the process of questioning or considering changing their sexual or gender identity.

Tranny/Trannie: Slur for transgender people. Reclaimed as a positive identity by some though this is relatively rare.

Transsexual: A slur to some, "transsexual" was the only word to describe people of the transgender experience before the term "transgender" came into use in the 1990s.

Advocates in 2010-2015 argued for "transgender" becoming the more widely used term in order to combat hyper-sexualization tactics from hate groups. Some have reclaimed the term as a positive identity and differentiate it from transgender as a way to indicate if one has had gender-affirming surgery to the genitals, though not all use the term this way.

Trans: Short for transgender. A transgender person has taken steps—socially, legally, medically, or a combination of all three—to change their gender identity and presentation to differ from the one assigned at birth.

Trans care: Umbrella term encompassing health and mental healthcare specifically for transgender people.

Trans man: A transgender man was assigned female at birth and now presents and identifies in a masculine way. A largely outdated term for this was "FTM" though some still identify with this term.

Trans person, trans people: Umbrella term for anyone who is not cisgender. It is often used to describe non-binary people who identify as trans or the trans and non-binary population as a whole.

Trans woman: A transgender woman was assigned male at birth and now presents and identifies in a feminine way. A largely outdated term for this was "MTF" though some still identify with this term.